OWN YOUR ZONE!

**What Students Need to Succeed
From School to Career**

OWN
YOUR
ZONE!

**A WAKE-UP CALL!
FOR PARENTS, STUDENTS & EDUCATORS**

Helene Naftali

Zone In Group

Published by Zone In Group, Wyckoff, NJ

ISBN 978-0-615-82274-7

Printed in the U.S.A.

Dedication

I am dedicating this book to my wonderful parents, Bernie and Shirley, for giving me the love and confidence to follow my dreams, to make a difference in the world, and to know that I can accomplish whatever I put my mind to.

Table of Contents

Foreword

This is an important book for our millennial generation and their future. Decisions made now by these up-and-coming leaders will surely impact not only their lives, but the lives of those with whom they will come in contact in every rank of society.

Helene Naftali accurately delineates the effects of thoughtful introspection on this new generation of aspiring college students. Her message is clear. Students need to find their own personal zone to maximize their future.

As a college professor, I encounter students who are in search of a second or even a third career. Many have reported dissatisfaction with careers in marketing, business, real estate, sales and even performing arts. The degrees they earned from their previous college experiences did not provide them with a sense of true satisfaction. Earning a good living was important and valuable, but each of these career-changing students wanted more. And, as difficult as it is, they are willing to pay for additional college courses to take them where their hearts and minds want them to be.

On a personal level, my daughter was graduated from college with a degree in business and went on to receive a master's degree in finance. The result of these efforts was a high-paying, prestigious position with a major Wall Street player. She was responsible for recommending the expenditure of hundreds of millions of dollars and met with the top elected officials of many states.

One day, in midst of all this success, she announced that this was not what she was meant to do and submitted her resignation. She explained that it was her calling, "her inner zone," to help others on a personal level. So, after twelve years in the business world, she left to study teaching.

Today she is a beloved elementary school teacher and community leader who receives a great sense of satisfaction by working with children every day. Had she more clearly examined her inner self with guidance from her parents and/or from experts, she would have had twenty-four years of contributions to society and greatly reduced the expenses incurred by extended educational requirements.

Helene Naftali has written an important book for the upcoming generation of aspiring young people. The many true examples portrayed in the book and the insightful, relevant quotations of famous minds should serve as an important road map for future generations to find their own true zones and calling.

Felix Berman
Senior Clinical Adjunct Professsor
Adelphi University
Garden City, New York

NOTE: Felix Berman is presently a Senior Clinical Adjunct Professor at Adelphi University. He previously served as principal, acting superintendent and deputy superintendent for the New York City Board of Education.

Preface

This book is about helping high-school and college-age students as well as recent graduates to "Own Their Zone." Their zone is where their unique gift (and they have one) intersects with what they would love to do or change in the world. When young adults have the opportunity to be guided through a process to figure out their zone before or early on during college, they can then spend their time in college intentionally testing, affirming and exploring their zone's applications. Learning their zone complements the significant growth that naturally occurs during the college years and can ensure that the college years are spent wisely. When they have completed the process, they will own their zone and will be able to sell themselves to future employers and clients.

The Current College Debate

For generations, Americans have viewed college as a ticket to a decent job and a happy life. There is, however, a fundamental shift afoot in the middle-class landscape in America today. A public debate has emerged over the value of a college degree given the high costs and the lack of jobs. As we go to print, there are headlines similar to these:

"If You Need a Job, Invent It"

"Do You Need College to Get a Job?"

"The Return on Investment of a College Education"

"Millennials are Redefining Work"

College is no longer automatically viewed as a good return on an investment as millennials struggle to find jobs even with degrees from prestigious universities. At the same time we see that a degree is not necessarily essential to success. The media continually glorifies those without a formal or traditional college education who skyrocket to fame and fortune thanks to the start-up and high-tech revolution.

Non-Traditional Students Also Need to Own Their Zone! (Maybe Even More!)

To be very clear, I believe that college is invaluable for knowledge, independence, personal growth, networking and, hopefully, learning how to get along with all types of people from diverse backgrounds. Students who are already on their way to "own their zone" while in college are particularly well positioned to use the college years constructively and to leave college clear and ready for the workforce. In many ways, this answers the questions about the value of college, the cost of college and the future student-debt burden. It is worth it *IF* the student discovers his or her zone and can begin to own it!

That being said, whether or not one goes to college, it is essential for him/her to know who he/she is and his/her one true zone. Those who choose a non-traditional approach to college must dig deep and learn who they are. Designing their own education and experience is a huge undertaking that requires self-awareness!

Students who take classes online, for example, and put together their own education, must be prepared for *how* to choose *what* to study. With so many choices available to them and fewer constraints of time, professors, or availability, these students need to discover or "own their zone" so that their work is done with desire, intentionality, and genuine interest. Owning their zone will give non-traditional young people the confidence necessary to sell themselves to future employers as they will have a more difficult challenge.

Passion as the Differentiator

Thanks to technology, in today's rapidly changing world, information and knowledge are now readily available at anyone's fingertips. This has leveled the playing field, making it even more important for young people to know themselves. What differentiates one smart person from another is the personal passion that individual exudes from doing what he or she loves.

Today, irrespective of their formal higher education, each student has to be a storyteller, prepared to tell his or her story to a potential employer. Employers are looking for passion, commitment and leadership qualities. Once young people know who they are and what they need in order to feel fulfilled and personally gain important insights about themselves, they will have the ability to tell their story and to sell themselves. Finding their one true zone is the starting place for their story: "Once I discovered x, y and z about myself, I then made these choices about my education and sought these experiences to complement and apply my studies." The passion and confidence they will emit when telling their story clearly will make a difference.

According to a 2010 study conducted by Intuit, a software company, by 2020 more than 40 percent of the U.S. workforce will likely be freelancers. This makes the ability to sell oneself even more important.

John Schlifske, the CEO of Northwestern Mutual, gave students at St. Louis University the following career advice, which was highlighted in the May 27, 2013, issue of *Forbes Magazine.* The article, "CEO Wisdom Heard From The Top," was written by Rich Karlgaard. This was Schlifske's advice:

This is a tough economy, but you can be successful if you do these four things: follow your passion, master your craft, study history and philosophy for leadership lessons, and live frugally.[1]

In an article he wrote for *Forbes Magazine,* Pierre Gergis, gave sound reasons why millennials with unconventional majors will be most welcomed and sought after in the corporate world.

They prioritize academic rigor, passion, enthusiasm, demonstrated achievement and leadership personalities. This thinking is sound and modern. Training can't make a person a good fit, but if you hire the right person, training can fill in the gaps and help them speak your company's language.[2]

The world is changing and moving fast. My message to all of us parents, educators, college counselors, coaches, therapists and admissions officers is that we need our children to "hurry up and slow down." This book is meant as a wake-up call and a plea that we help slow things down enough so that young people can learn about themselves, ideally *before* they embark on a path towards higher education. Let's guide them towards a course that will lead to success, whatever that looks like for each of them.

Helene Naftali

Be an untouchable, do what you love. This is not sappy career advice but an absolute survival strategy, because as I like to put it the world is getting flat.... The flatter the world gets, the more essential it is that you do what you love, because all the boring, repetitive jobs that remain are those that cannot be automated or outsourced; they are jobs that demand or encourage some uniquely human creative flair, passion, and imagination. In other words, jobs that can be done only by people who love what they do...

~ Thomas Friedman

INTRODUCTION
An Aha! Moment*

Lynn Cooper was ready to pull out her hair. Her daughter Blake had been home for only two days on spring break from college and already Lynn and her only child were revisiting a familiar topic of aggravation.

"You can't be serious," Lynn said, carefully negotiating through the heavy late afternoon traffic. "You want to do *what* one more time?"

"Change my major."

"I thought you loved psychology."

"Psychology doesn't grab me anymore. It doesn't really interest me."

"So, what do you want to earn your degree in now?"

"I was thinking maybe art history," Blake replied.

"And what happens to the classes you've already taken?"

"Some of the credits would apply to the change. Most of them wouldn't."

"So, basically, you would be starting from scratch."

"You don't have to sound so negative, Mom."

*This *could* be a true story.

1

"The only negative will be in my checking account. There's no way you can switch majors again and still graduate in four years."

"I know, but I'm not happy studying psychology."

"And switching to art history will make you happy?"

"I'm positive."

"Isn't that what you said when you switched from political science to psychology?" Lynn bit her tongue and focused on the traffic ahead. "How can you be so certain, Blake?"

"It just seems right this time, Mom. Trust me."

Lynn wanted to help set her daughter on the right career path, but she had no idea how to truly help her. Not knowing what else she could say to Blake at this point, she just let it go, at least for the moment.

"Tell me again why we're going today?" Blake asked, eager to talk about something else.

"When you were born, I put in a request for extra maternity leave; initially that request was denied. Because of Mr. Golden's intervention—I was his assistant at the time—I was able to take off eight weeks without losing my job. Going today is my way of acknowledging his help."

"That was a long time ago, Mom. He probably doesn't even remember you."

"Of course he does, honey."

Lynn signaled for a left, turned into the entrance for Solomon Electric's number one plant, and was soon through the security gate and parking the car. Moments later Lynn and her daughter stood outside the door where a security guard named David waved them inside.

"We're not too late, are we?" Lynn asked.

David shook his head. "No, not too late at all."

After forty-three years, six months, three weeks, two days, sixteen hours, thirty-three minutes and seventeen seconds, the time for Jack Golden's retirement party had arrived. In honor of the occasion, and at no small expense, the entire office complex had closed an hour early so that everyone employed at the company could unite in celebrating Jack Golden's remarkable career. Lynn and Blake joined the crowd of close to five hundred men and women who were waiting for the festivities to begin.

Richard Solomon, the current owner of the family-run business, approached podium on the makeshift stage that had been erected less than an hour before. "Good afternoon, ladies and gentlemen," Richard Solomon spoke into the podium's microphone. "Welcome, as we pay tribute to Jack Golden, a man who has devoted more than four decades of his life to ensuring that Solomon Electric is nothing less than the finest provider of electrical solutions in the known universe." Enthusiastic applause rippled through the factory.

Richard Solomon went on, "It goes without saying that we are all richer for Jack Golden's extraordinary contribution to this company, which all of us are proud to call home." More spontaneous applause erupted, accompanied by concentrated pockets of cheers and whistles. Richard Solomon held up his hands and smiled. "But enough jabbering from me. It's my pleasure to present the Man of the Hour, your friend and mine, Mr. Jack Golden."

The applause had been substantial, but now, as Jack Golden climbed the steps to the stage, the crowd, including Lynn, went wild. That Jack's pace was much slower than it had been for many years was apparent to all, but given his loyal, dedicated service over many years in Solomon Electric, this slower pace was to be expected. Jack paused long enough to shake Richard Solomon's hand.

The crowd settled down, and Jack Golden began to speak. "Thank you. Thank you." Jack's eyes swept over the sea of faces before him. "And thanks to Richard for such a wonderful introduction."

Richard Solomon waved graciously from the sidelines.

"I couldn't have imagined so long ago," Jack said, his voice sounding more than a little bit weary, "that I would one day be standing before you actually about to retire. A man of my years has had ample time for reflection, and what I am about to say will probably surprise you. As a matter of fact, it surprises me. In many ways I feel like a prisoner who's just had his life sentence commuted by the governor." Jack smiled as laughter danced across the factory floor.

"My entry into Solomon Electric was unremarkable. I was a few weeks away from graduating from college and I knew I had to find a job. Learning about Solomon involved precious little research on my part. Likewise, I didn't do any soul-searching to determine whether I would be a good fit for Solomon or if Solomon would be a good fit for me.

"My first contact with Solomon Electric came about because a friend of a friend of a friend—I really don't remember who it was—happened to mention that Solomon was hiring. Next thing I knew, I was interviewing for an entry-level position in the quality-control department, and now here I am, forty-plus years later, about to be put out to pasture."

Jack's eyes shifted from left to right as he leaned into the microphone. His voice lowered to an amplified whisper. "I'll let you in on a little secret: The life we celebrate today acknowledging my dedicated devotion to Solomon Electric isn't really what you think it is. But what I am about to share is the truth. Every day for more than forty years—while I totally appreciated the opportunity and support I got—I dreaded coming to work. And why? Simple. I have always been unhappy at my job."

A collective gasp, perhaps the loudest coming from Richard Solomon, reverberated throughout the factory.

"It didn't matter where I worked in the company—sales, customer service, human resources or management—it was and always has been the same. I never looked forward to going to work.

5

"Don't get me wrong," Jack quickly countered. "I'm not at all saying Solomon Electric is a bad company just because I personally did not like working here. In fact, it's just the opposite! I have worked with and made some of the best friends a man could ever hope for through Solomon. The blame for my discontent rests entirely with me...and all because no matter what I did within the confines of Solomon Electric, I never enjoyed it.

"I know what some of you must be thinking: Old Jack Golden is crazy. He made a small fortune each year. He owns three homes. And we've never seen him drive a car more than a year old. Surely, Jack Golden has every reason in the world to be deliriously happy. What a bitter, ungrateful guy he must be to have so much and appreciate it so little. What on earth is wrong with this guy?

"The harsh truth is that my financial success came at a terrible cost. Because I slavishly devoted my life to Solomon Electric, I have a son and a daughter who grew up rarely seeing their father. I was always too busy working to spend time with them. I regret those lost years, and yet I have duplicated the same error with my grandchildren. To them, I'm almost a stranger."

Jack Golden visibly trembled from head to toe. He composed himself as he brought his speech to an emotional, heartfelt conclusion. "I don't want to appear ungrateful for all Solomon has offered me. Neither do I want to be a downer at my own retirement celebration. I thought long and hard about this speech, and my point is not to ruin the afternoon, but to share these personal reflections in the hope that I can prevent others from making the same mistakes.

"Starting before I left high school, or at least early on in college, I should have done anything and everything within my power to find out enough about myself to ensure that I would choose a career path that would lead to happiness as well as financial success. I should have left no stone unturned in my search for a profession that nurtured my soul, left me smiling at the end of the day, and gave me the personal satisfaction of being able to spend quality time with my family. I should have done whatever I had to do—no matter how long it took or how hard I had to work—to make it happen. If I could do it over again, my life would be very different, indeed."

Blake looked at her mother and sighed, "That's going to be me if I stick with psychology."

"I wish I knew how to help you," her mother replied sincerely. "You can't just keep changing majors. There has to be a better way."

"Excuse me, but I couldn't help overhearing," said a man standing next to them. He handed Lynn a business card. "My own daughter just completed a coaching process that guided her in the direction of finding a career path that is the right one for her. It started with her choice of the right college and the right major. As a college student, the self-exploration enabled her to take a step back, figure out who she really is, what she would love to do, and what she is meant to do, so she can be happy AND successful at work."

Lynn looked at her daughter and then reached for her cell phone.

Blake asked, "Whom are you calling, Mom?"

Lynn nodded in the direction of the man who had given her the card. "You heard the man. We need to find out more about this coaching process!"

Blake hugged her mother with gratitude and affection. "Thanks, Mom! I get it! That *really* is what I need."

CHAPTER ONE

Navigating the College and Career Decisions Maze

> One person with passion is better than forty people merely interested. Loving what you do is like winning the lottery. It means that on most mornings getting up and getting going is relatively easy. It means that you aren't leading Thoreau's life of quiet desperation, or trapped in an Edward Hopper painting going through the motions in a sepia-toned fog, feeling isolated and despondent.
>
> ~ E.M. Forester

No one deliberately sets off on a journey intending to get lost along the way. With a clear-cut destination in mind, expectations for successfully getting from Point A to Point B run high. When preparation and planning prior to departure fail to take into account all the necessary variables for staying on course, however, Point B may never be reached. Or even if it is, it may turn out that Point B is not where you should have been heading in the first place.

This is especially true when the decision-making process involves seeking a higher education and choosing a career. A miscalculation anywhere along the journey holds the potential to transform good intentions into mishaps. The repercussions from these unintentional missteps, both financial and emotional, can last a lifetime.

According to an August 2012 Gallup Poll, the majority of workers in the United States (53%) are either dissatisfied or only somewhat satisfied with their job. Another Gallup Poll, which was taken throughout 2012, shows that over 70% of people in the United States say that they are either "not engaged" or "actively disengaged" in their work! **That means that less than one-third of Americans are involved in and enthusiastic about their work.**

This situation repeats itself with millions of college students over and over, year after year. It begins from the time they leave school and lasts throughout their lives. There are two major reasons this keeps happening:

- People tend to focus on how they can make the most money, regardless of how much they may enjoy what they will do.

- The career exploration process is largely nonexistent.

Let's concentrate on the Career Exploration Process first.

******

The Career Exploration Process

There are three major steps to take from high school to the world of careers, but only two of those steps are carefully designed for you. The first step is a clear process to determine which college you will attend.

There are college planners to assist those who can afford the help. Additionally, you can learn a great deal about colleges you are interested in on your own. You can request brochures or related promotional materials, and there is an abundance of information available on the internet. There is also the option of visiting colleges to see how they feel to you, what the campus atmosphere is like, and how the school's curriculum options support your goals for higher education. School visits also provide the opportunity to explore the diversity of the student population.

College affords you the opportunity to take different classes so you can begin to sense what might interest you. Next thing you know, you must declare a major. Once that necessity kicks in, the pressure becomes unbearable, regardless of whether or not you know what you want to do, what you would love to do, or what you are meant to do.

It is so easy to get caught up in the process of declaring a major—to fall like Alice sliding down the rabbit hole, tumbling into the abyss, backed into a corner, making one of the most important decisions of your life without any real understanding of *why* you are making it. Too often you discover too late that in surrendering to the onslaught of ill-researched reasons, the path you have taken is the totally wrong path for you.

The third step in the career-exploration process involves the systematic approach to finding work once you have decided what you want to do with the rest of your life. Most colleges have career-counseling centers that provide advice and numerous resources to show you how to write a résumé, what to say and what not to say during an interview, where and when to send résumés and cover letters, how and when to follow up, and so on.

But what about the second step? How will you discover what it is that you would love to do? **Where can you turn so you will know without question what you are destined to do,** what will make your heart sing, day in and day out? What changes would you absolutely love to see in the world, so important to you that you jump at the chance to be part of the transformation? Where is the clear method to enable you to immerse yourself in a career that will have you waking up Monday mornings with a sense of excitement, anticipation and fulfillment, chomping at the bit to have your new week up and running?

For some recent graduates, this means floundering from career to career, scrounging to find work that is satisfying and pays the bills. For many it means just trying to get any job—often settling for a job that does not require a college degree. For others it means attending graduate school, an acceptable way to take a break from the grind while finding the time to reflect.

******

Money Isn't Everything

Don't let money be your mantra. Focusing only on financial success often leaves you with a big bank account and a barren soul.

~ E.M. Forester

Focusing on which profession will bring you the most money virtually ensures that you will end up joining the ranks of the 70% of people polled by Gallup who are not enthusiastic about their jobs. Don't fall into the trap of choosing a career path based solely on potential earnings. Studies show that **making the amount of money you think you can earn your first priority at the expense of considering options that reflect what you would really love to do can negatively impact your potential for both success *and* happiness.** There is a high correlation between success and earnings that goes hand in hand with choosing the emotionally sustainable career that is right for you.

If you elect to choose the money route first, what is the probability that you will be courageous enough to change careers if it becomes obvious that you have made a terrible mistake? What then? Imagine how much harder it will be to shift gears once you have a family and responsibilities beyond yourself. The mind boggles.

Many will begin their grueling climb, advancing up the "ladder of success" in a job or industry they don't like. After a few years, they would like to make a change to more satisfying work, but they realize it is too late. This disturbing scenario repeats itself again and again.

13

Percentage of People Engaged/Disengaged in Their Work

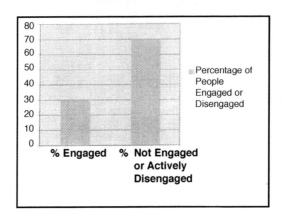

Gallup Poll:

These findings are the result of a special Gallup Daily tracking series conducted since the fourth quarter of 2010 to determine the engagement level of American workers.

The College Debt Crisis

Today's post-college landscape is particularly troubling given the exorbitant and rising cost of college and the problem of student debt. Four years of college can run as much as $108,000 and for some, way beyond. Now consider the fact that the average college student currently spends nearly six years completing a four-year program, adding tens of thousands of dollars to the cost. Factor in the possibility of graduate school, and it is easy to see how the price tag of higher education could skyrocket well above one's original budget!

The steep and rising cost of college takes a terrible toll on students and families across the country. Students who took out loans and graduated in 2012 left college with an average debt of about $24,257. Sadly, many of these graduates will still be paying off their student loans when the time comes for their own children to go to college. Is it any wonder Americans now owe more on student loans than on credit cards?

The reality is this: **Too many students take out tens of thousands of dollars in loans to finance their college and graduate education only to realize how ill-prepared they are to survive in the post-graduate landscape.** When preparation fails to meet the demand of reality, inevitably four possible outcomes emerge—none of them good:

- The student comes out of college unemployable. This is the worst outcome.

- The student comes out of college choosing an unsuitable career direction. He or she spends the next ten years miserably floundering about, trying to figure out what to do to change the situation. The lucky few change direction and start over.

- The student comes out of college and chooses a career path that doesn't excite him/her. Unfortunately, it is impossible to change course because of financial and familial responsibilities.

- The student comes out of college and chooses a career path that doesn't excite him/her. The student would like to change course but doesn't have a clue as to which direction to take.

Going through a guided self-discovery process serves as "protection" against the status quo of what's happening to these young people. Think of a child going to school facing the possibility of catching measles. Is it possible that the child might not get the disease even if he or she had not been inoculated against it? Of course. Nevertheless, most would agree that it is worth having the protection if they consider the risks and what is at stake.

Parents face a similar situation when it comes to helping their children make the most of their education and protecting them from possibly wasting ten years or more making the same the mistakes that plague so many graduates. **Many believe that if they can just get their youngsters into a good college, they'll be fine. A better way to think about it is this: If we can get our children into college prepared to use the knowledge and experiences they will gain to successfully launch out into life, they'll be fine.**

16

Total Cost for 4, 5 or 6 Years of College

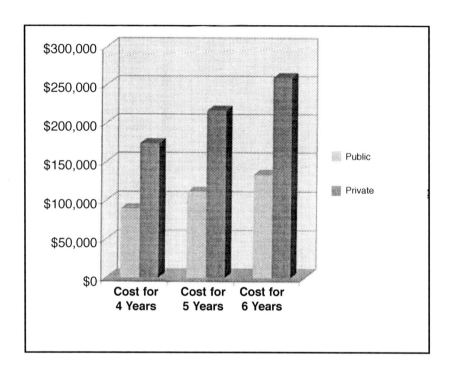

Average Cost Per Year:
Public College: $22,261
Private College: $43,289

NOTE: The data for this graph comes from The College Board's Trends in College Pricing, 2012-2013.

The Emotional Toll
of the Wrong Career Choice

Being uncertain and unhappy in a chosen career is hardly new. For years, people have graduated college without a clear sense of what they wanted to do; they have bounced between jobs and careers and reported being unhappy in their choices. This unhappiness is especially disturbing when you consider that most people will spend almost a third of their adult lives in the workplace. **Research has shown that job satisfaction is the single most important determining factor for life satisfaction and well-being.**

Of course, anyone who has had the experience of being dissatisfied in a job knows this firsthand. Odds are high that you can relate to this feeling of not enjoying your work. Most of us have experienced a time when simply getting through the week was a chore—a time when we felt sapped of energy and struggled to meet the responsibilities and commitments across multiple areas of life: family, friends, relationships, exercise and routine errands. As anyone who has suffered under these conditions can attest, being dissatisfied at work can have serious emotional implications and can impact your basic experience of life.

* * * * * *

So, the best advice to young people is to get it right the first time. Due to the collective uncertainty that defines being in your twenties, it is generally accepted that this is the period of life to figure things out. The self-knowledge gained at the start of this incredible journey can empower young men and women to pursue an education and career path that both reflects and honors their uniqueness.

Danger Signs that You Are in the Wrong Career or Job

- You don't like to talk about what you do.

- You can't wait for Friday to arrive.

- You are not excited or upbeat about going to work each day.

- You live for the weekends and experience dread on Sunday nights.

- You would change your path if only you just knew how to do it.

- You feel unchallenged, bored or frustrated at work.

Mel Zuckerman, wellness expert and founder of the spa Canyon Ranch, wrote about the emotional implications of being in the wrong career in *Mel's Tips for Healthy Living:*

> Many times, the grinding, serious stress in people's lives arises from a mismatch between their values—what they love and need—and the way they live. The man who loves human contact and conversation but is holed up alone in an office all day needs to change his life; so does the woman who values family above all else but works crazy hours.

19

Sometimes the only cure for persistent, chronic stress is to make substantial changes....If you're carrying a great deal of stress that's arising from a fundamental conflict between your values and your daily life, seriously explore how you can fix it.[3]

Being in the wrong job causes stress and has implications for your well-being and your health. Statistics show that this is a way of life for the vast majority of Americans. Some people say, "Work is work. You're not supposed to like it." **But when you talk to people who are wildly successful *and* happy in their work, they will tell you that for them, work is literally play and that loving their work actually *enabled* their success.**

The Benefits of Being Passionate about Your Work

Being passionate about your work adds value to what you have to offer and boosts your chances for success. When your work is aligned with your inner nature, you are excited to get out of bed every morning. You are driven, living with purpose and intention—even urgency. You experience a natural, unlimited high.

Author and coach Brendon Burchard talks about the benefit of being "pulled by a calling" versus the hard work of having to push yourself to get out of bed and through the day. Who do you think will have a better chance for success—the person pulled by his or her calling or the person who struggles to do the work every day?

Another way to think about being passionate and engaged in your work is to compare it to riding a bike down a gently sloping hill versus pedaling uphill. Biking downhill is almost effortless, while biking uphill requires a constant struggle to make headway. When you love what you do, your progress and productivity day to day can be automatic, requiring minimal effort. Although struggling is sometimes required, you are still pulled in during those moments by the sense of passion and purpose of what you are doing.

Loving your work also makes you a more effective salesperson—even if it is selling yourself! Passion coupled with enthusiasm is a very appealing quality. It can give you a real edge on the job and in interviews. The person who is passionate, positive and enthusiastic will more often than not get the job over the person who chooses the job just because of money. The worker who loves his job will also be better able to win clients and to earn the respect and support of his coworkers.

Think about something you believe in deeply or are passionate about: a product, a service, or an experience you have had. Have you ever talked someone into doing something because you loved it? You know the passion and quality of energy that you brought to that encounter. When you carry that natural passion to your work—when you really believe and care about what you are doing—you are bound to be more productive and effective.

These icons of success know that loving what you do is critical to being successful.

Do what you would do if you were in my position, where the money means nothing to you. At 79, I work every day. And it's what I want to do more than anything else in the world. The closer you can come to that early on in your life, you know the more fun you're going to have in life and really the better you're going to do. So don't be driven where you think the last dollar is presently or anything of that sort. Go to work at a job that turns you on.

~ Warren Buffett

I never went into business just to make money. I found that if I have fun, the money will come. I often ask myself, is my work fun and does it make me happy? I believe that the answer to that is more important than fame or fortune. If it stops being fun, I ask why? If I can't fix it, I stop doing it.

~ Richard Branson

You know you are on the road to success if you would do your job and not be paid for it.

~ Oprah Winfrey

Consider this for a moment: How many people do you know who do extremely well but are engaged in a profession that does not excite them? On the other hand, how many people do you know who followed their gut instincts—their inner drive—and are both happy and successful in their career?

Greg's Story: An Intern's "Realization on a Train"

"This summer I worked at an internship that had me doing mindless work in New York City for eight hours a day. Although I am grateful to have had the work experience, I did not really learn that much in the workplace besides some knowledge about employee relations. With that said, taking the job actually provided the opportunity to learn my most valuable lesson of the summer.

"Every morning I had to catch the 7:17 train to Hoboken and then transfer to the Path into the city. What struck me the most were the expressions that many of the passengers on these trains had on their faces. I sat next to many men and women who looked truly miserable. They were obviously dreading the day that was ahead of them, knowing that this experience would repeat itself for days, weeks and, most likely, years to come.

"It bothered me that so many people appear to drudgingly endure work that is unfulfilling and sometimes unpleasant for such a large portion of their lives. Seeing these seemingly miserable people motivated me to determine my own true passion and to find a way to do it for a living. Having an enjoyable job is such an important part of life. I feel really lucky to have had this realization on the train."

* * * * * *

Michele's Story: A Successful Consultant

Long before she had her current consulting business, as an undergraduate Michele worked in her family business but did not enjoy it. It was during this time that she attended graduate school at night, where she discovered her passion for consulting and solving problems.

Michele's father had always stressed that monetary considerations should come first when choosing a career. Liking what you do placed a distant second at best. Michele disagreed, which typically led to arguments, but Michele wasn't swayed to change her mind.

Michele recognized early on her necessity to love what she did and has always stayed true to that belief. She knew that in order to maintain her happiness, money would have to take a backseat to doing what she enjoys. Working as a consultant and problem solver has certainly lived up to Michele's expectations.

She sums up her feelings this way: "It's essential for young people to find a passion and follow it, to learn from their experiences and to be open to new things in order to focus in on what they truly love."

* * * * * *

W. Howard Lester:
Chairman of Williams Sonoma (1935-2010)

Loving Your Work, published by Harvard Business Press, contains a number of interviews of renowned business leaders. One of those leaders is W. Howard Lester, Chairman of Williams Sonoma. In the book, Lester described his feelings about his career. His remarks exemplify the importance of doing what you love:

> One of the main conclusions I reached was that...this is not a dress rehearsal and I wanted to do things that I loved doing....If I were doing things I loved, then I would have a better chance at being good at it than doing something that I didn't love....I can tell you that over the last twenty-seven years, I don't think there's ever been a day or a morning I wasn't excited about getting up and going to work.[4]

* * * * * *

Decide Early

If loving what you do adds value to what you have to offer and boosts your chances of success, so does having clarity about who you are and the work that is best for you as soon as possible. We often talk about the cost of college but seldom pay attention to the hidden costs of getting on the wrong career path after graduation.

Eric Sinoway, president & co-founder of Axcess Worldwide and author of *You're Probably Not Very Good at Most Things,* stressed this importance of making career decisions sooner rather than later. "The hard reality is that most of us have few areas in which we really, truly excel," noted Sinoway. "The key is to identify those areas and then to search for professional opportunities where our strongest capacities are most often needed and utilized. The earlier in your career that you identify these, the easier it is for you to take control over your own professional trajectory."[5]

Rachel Brown, director of the career center at Temple University in Philadelphia, pointed out that a person changes careers three to five times on average. "And while median salary is certainly something students should be aware of," she added, "it shouldn't be the deciding factor. Take that into consideration, but look at the whole picture. What are you doing every day? What are the job responsibilities? What are the values of the occupation in general? What is the advancement potential?"[6]

It is crucial to learn as soon as possible what your gift to the world is. Tying that knowledge to your chosen career path will set the stage for you to be a winner.

Two Career-Path Scenarios:
One Works...The Other Doesn't

Person A graduates college unclear about what he wants to do and enters into work he doesn't like. When he turns 28, he gets a much clearer idea about what he wants to do and takes a job in a completely different industry; however, he has to start at a much lower position than the one he held in his previous job.

Person B gained a clear understanding about who she is and the career path she is suited for while still in college. She sought out this work as part of her job search in her senior year and chose an industry based on this knowledge. She continues to focus on meeting people in this industry, gaining skills and experience and advancing efficiently on her career path.

Compare the difference in the quality of the experiences for these two people. Person A, although now in an area that is right for him, is not totally satisfied with his situation because he lags behind where he would have been if he had known from the start that this is where he belonged. Person B, on the other hand, feels good about herself and the knowledge that she correctly identified her calling—her ideal career path. It is likely that Person B will produce at a much higher pace than Person A, taking Person B to greater heights and more success.

Think about Person A's career path as being similar to choosing the wrong train. If you get on the D train (a job in industry X), but you belong on the A train (a job in industry Y), you might find yourself in Queens when you should be in Brooklyn.

You have to come all the way back to get to where you're supposed to be! The only problem is that now you are twenty-five or thirty—perhaps you're married, maybe you have kids—and you have responsibilities and expenses. How do you go back? For many people, you don't.

* * * * * *

Two Sides of the "Career Choices" Coin

Side One

My colleagues and I have talked with many adults who told this same story: They learned the hard way the costs associated with years of uncertainty before finally "figuring it out"—if they ever did at all. These people so wished they had had the self-awareness needed to apply their special qualities to career choices. (See Chapter Four: Too Little Too Late—the Risks of Not Planning.)

Many of these adults graduated college with a "well-rounded" education. After graduation they stumbled into a first job and then into a second job, which allowed them to pay their bills. Next thing they knew, they were approaching middle age and wondering how on earth they wound up doing what they're doing. They wished they had taken a different path, but realized that at this point they couldn't jump off the merry-go-round because they needed the money.

One of these people was a businessman named Gary. Gary ended up in a business-related career because he realized that he had a natural affinity for math. What kept him from moving to a different path once he began to feel dissatisfied with his chosen route was the money he was making. This proved to be an impossible obstacle to circumvent.

Gary explained, "I went for the big bucks right from the start. This blinded me from ever questioning if I would be passionate about my work or even if I would enjoy my chosen career. True, I make a lot of money, but I'm not at peace at all. It's been like this ever since I left school. I was so driven to be successful and to pull in the cash that I never thought of anything else. I never had a process to help me figure out what I was doing.

"To take a step back, switch careers and live a different lifestyle, it was something I just couldn't do," admitted Gary. "It's hard to get off the fast track, especially when you factor in your family responsibilities and how much it costs to survive. "I truly wish I had learned, before it was too late, what worked for me. There are many ways to find financial success. It would be great to do it with passion and enjoyment."

Side Two

On the flip side of that coin, I also spoke with adults who were wildly successful and happy. **They attributed their success to having the self-knowledge and confidence that gave them the insight to know which career path to follow.** This clarity enabled them to engage in life with intention, to take ownership of the direction of their lives, and to create the lifestyle and the financial rewards they now enjoy.

One such individual is Dr. Mark Liponis, whose parents were aware early on that their son was a strong, well-rounded student with a particular strength in the sciences. With parental guidance, Mark took high school AP (Advanced Placement) classes in the sciences so that from the time he enrolled in college he was able to take courses that reflected his ability. As a result, Dr. Liponis learned early in his college career not only that he was *strong* in science, but also that he was very *interested in* and excited by the field. He did his homework! This led Mark to major in biology and ultimately to pursue a career in medicine.

However, Mark also knew that his *greatest* gift is his ability to empathize with people. His career as the Corporate Medical Director at Canyon Ranch is a great marriage of his strength and interest in science and his gift of empathy. This winning combination has led to both a successful career and personal fulfillment.

* * * * * *

Road Blocks and Speed Bumps

Despite the proven value of loving what you do and of having self-knowledge and awareness early on, **far too many college students continue to graduate without any true sense of direction,** setting themselves up for the very real possibility of an unfulfilling career and an unrealized life. What gets in their way? Why do they have trouble finding clarity about the type of work that will lead to satisfying careers?

Part of that uncertainty is due to the fact that with every generation there is more and more to learn. This is intensified against a backdrop of increased specialization. As employment grows more complicated, more preparation is required to even begin to compete for jobs that exist.

College students must make viable strategic decisions—decisions that will impact their lives for years to come. Without the proper tools to assist them, making the appropriate decisions is difficult. Most don't have the experience to know what makes a good or bad choice because they haven't yet tested the waters of the real world. To keep them from drowning, we need to equip students with as much self-knowledge as possible. Only then will they begin to possess the necessary tools to survive once they graduate.

Certainly, colleges provide tremendous opportunities for exploration both of self and of career. Students gain knowledge on a wide array of subjects and are able to meet with professors and mentors. Colleges can connect students with internships, and career counselors offer resources for job exploration, résumé honing, interview preparation and networking. What's more, for students living away from home for the first time, the college years are a lesson in independence. All of these resources are valuable and support an environment where students can explore their particular abilities and learn how these qualities apply to potential careers.

Even with these positive conditions in place, however, many still graduate clueless about what to do next. **What is missing from high-school and college guidance programs is a way to help students clarify their career goals *before* graduating from college—preferably before choosing a major—instead of "figuring it out" afterward.** What is needed is a guided process for determining what career path to choose in order to "love what you do" and find success in today's world.

My colleagues and I asked several young people and their parents how they arrived at their career choices. Similar explanations were given time and time again:

- It's what my parent(s) did.
- My parent(s) thought I should do it.
- I wanted to make money.
- I was good at a related subject, so I thought it would be a good choice.
- Somebody told me it was a great career.
- The recruiter came to campus.
- I heard that it was the up-and-coming career—where the jobs are.

When these same people discovered that a guided process exists for helping students learn their unique qualities in order to choose a career path that is best for them, many confessed that they wished they had been offered the opportunity to benefit from this process.

The man who starts out simply with the idea of getting rich won't succeed; you must have a larger ambition.

~ John D Rockefeller

There is no greatness without a passion to be great, whether it's the aspiration of an athlete or an artist, a scientist, a parent, or a businessperson.

~ Anthony Robbins

******

You Need to Know:
What Is Your One True Gift?

A critical component of "getting clear" about yourself and determining the work that is best for you, as well as getting the job, is knowing your "one unique gift." **Your gift describes your natural way of processing your experience—the natural, repeated way you relate to the world.** This concept that everyone has one special gift has been known across cultures, faiths and traditions throughout history; however, few people attempt to identify their own true gift.

Knowing this process for yourself is literally your power. It is so significant that in combination with your passions, talents and other vital components of your inner nature it can change everything. Going into an interview with this knowledge, you are able to advocate for yourself from a place of deep knowledge and truth; your language naturally reflects inner strength and confidence.

Self-knowledge plus direction plus confidence are crucial in differentiating oneself from others and being successful. However, most high schools and colleges fail to provide the guided, meaningful self-exploration necessary to uncover students' special abilities. Adding a guided process to help them engage in this exploration would be very beneficial. It would give students the necessary direction to take them down a career path, enabling choices that eventually lead to a career that uses their one unique gift and provides fulfillment and enjoyment to their working lives.

Unfortunately, several factors discourage young people from cultivating the critical self-knowledge they need for a foundation of career clarity in college. The hyper-structured, hyper-supervised environment in which we raise our children reflects a shift away from discovery and play and discourages the kind of self-knowledge our young adults need to navigate the treacherous waters of the real world.

Another factor is the emphasis on doing only what will help you get into a good college. In high school, students are encouraged to mold themselves in the image of an ideal college applicant, instead of who they really are. Instead of telling them to discover and pursue the activities they love, they hear, "Pursue the activities that make you appear 'well rounded' and that show achievement so that you can get into college."

In an article appearing in the Spring 2011 edition of *American Journal of Play*, author and psycologist Peter Gray, Professor Emeritus, Ph.D., at Boston College lamented the current state of play time reserved for today's kids. "Since about 1955, children's free play has been continually declining, at least partly because adults have exerted ever-increasing control over children's activities."[7]

Gray defines "free play" as play a child undertakes on his or her own, which is self-directed and an end in itself, rather than part of some organized activity. He views this type of freely chosen play as a testing ground for life, providing critical life experiences without which young children cannot develop into confident and competent adults.

Gray views the lack of childhood free play time as a great loss that must be addressed for the sake of our children and society. "Play time gives children a chance to find and develop a connection to their own self-identified and self-guided interests."

Gray cited several studies that indicate that there has been a significant increase in anxiety and depression from 1950 to the present day in teens and young adults. According to one of them, "Five to eight times as many children and college students reported clinically significant depression or anxiety than fifty years ago." Gray suggests that the loss of play is likely a factor in this rise; one reason for this is that play helps children learn how to handle emotions.

Suicide rates also climbed both for children under fifteen years of age and for teens and young adults. Gray feels the loss of unstructured, free play for play's sake is at the core of this alarming increase. He argues that "without play, young people fail to acquire the social and emotional skills necessary for healthy psychological development."[8]

When we engage in what we are naturally suited to do, our work takes on the quality of play and it is play that stimulates creativity.

~ Linda Naiman

David Brooks, columnist for the *New York Times,* also pointed out the cost of substituting free play with play time with excessive supervision:

> This year's graduates are members of the most supervised generation in American history. Through their childhoods and teenage years, they have been monitored, tutored, coached and honed to an unprecedented degree. Yet upon graduation they will enter a world that is unprecedentedly wide open and unstructured. Most of them will not quickly get married, buy a home and have kids, as previous generations did.
>
> Instead, they will confront amazingly diverse job markets, social landscapes and lifestyle niches. Most will spend a decade wandering from job to job and clique to clique, searching for a role.
>
> No one would design a system of extreme supervision to prepare people for a decade of extreme openness. But this is exactly what has emerged in modern America.[9]

* * * * * *

It's Time to Get Serious

Aspects of the college experience today suggest that many students are not using the college years productively. Signs of this include increased partying, a greater number of students who switch majors, and the fact that many students are taking more than four years to graduate. **Studies showing limited learning on campus bring into question the function of college as a means to prepare students for the role they are meant to play in the real world.**

Imagine this alternative: Instead of a "five-year party," as author Craig Brandon calls it in the title of his book, **college could be a clear process leading to clarity and direction.** It would include taking academic classes, **having mentor experiences and cultivating relationships with professors.** At the same time students would be **shadowing, networking and meeting with people in different fields.** The result would be that after four years, students would not only graduate with a degree and a major, they would also start out on a career path that is right for them.

This crucial work can and should begin *before college.* We need to fundamentally change the way our kids approach institutions of higher learning. Students must use the college experience in a way that will help them determine the role they are best suited for in the real world—a way that will empower them to engage in their courses and experiences with intention. This means that students would look at the four years of college as an opportunity to clarify their role in the real world, as opposed to continually switching majors, not planning, and graduating without clear direction.

Taking Responsibility

Accomplishing the goal of a meaningful college experience is not only the responsibility of students; it is also the responsibility of parents. It begins by giving young people the opportunity to engage in meaningful self-exploration and to clarify their singular role in the world. It means encouraging them to set themselves on a career path that will give them the best chance for success and satisfaction.

We must provide the preparation and guidance needed to make the most of their college experience so they enter the real world with the clarity and confidence needed to secure a job in today's economy. The process is an investment, one that we cannot afford to ignore. If we do, we will be paying for it many times over in the form of wasted time, unnecessary debt, and missed opportunities for success and satisfaction in our children's lives.

People who are passionate about their work are happier, more fulfilled and more likely to be financially successful, no matter what their career path may be. Test this theory out for yourself. Examine your own job satisfaction and the job satisfaction of some of your friends and relatives: Who is happy in their work? Who is financially successful? Who is counting the days to retirement? Who will be happy to work well into old age? Undoubtedly, you'll see a correlation between work satisfaction and financial success!

KEY POINTS

1. More than 70% of people in the United States are not enthusiastic about their jobs.

2. Many people focus first on how they can make the most money, regardless of how much they may like or love what they will do.

3. The career-exploration process is almost nonexistent.

4. Many students take more than four years to complete a four-year program, adding tens of thousands of dollars to the cost of higher education.

5. A self-exploration process is missing!

CHAPTER TWO

An Exploration of One's Unique Gift as It Naturally Plays Out

What I know for sure from this experience with you is that we are called—everyone has a calling—and your real job in life is to figure out what that is and gets about the business of doing it.

~ Oprah Winfrey

Throughout history, people of different cultures and traditions have said that every person has one unique "gift." People in various cultures just call it by different names. Your gift is not a skill or a talent, like writing, singing or being good with numbers. It is the distinctive lens through which you see the world—your personal framework for processing everything in your experience. Your gift is the natural way you relate to the world. It is the process describing what you naturally look for in every encounter, interaction and situation.

Even as you read this sentence, your gift is at work. Naturally, your mind is looking for something, and this process is yours and exclusive to you. For example, a student named Sam discovered that her gift was "finding truth." When she reads a book, Sam boils down every bit of written information to its most basic essential truth so that she can thoroughly evaluate it and discover what is really true.

Whatever your gift is, whatever this process or lens is for you, it is the same process that you use, and have used, to process everything in your life. You don't choose it. It is just part of you. When you were sitting in class, you were filtering what you heard and saw through this lens which you alone possess. At the same time everyone else in the room was using his or her own particular process. You naturally looked for one thing. The person sitting next to you was looking for something totally different.

Your gift is at the core of the way you engage with the world, all of the time. It is the beautiful, singular way you participate: the essence of your way. It is also your "genius" because this process is not only your "way," it is also something that you do better than everyone else. You are a GENIUS at your process, and you do it naturally!

If one advances confidently in the direction of his dreams, and endeavors to live the life which he had imagined, he will meet with a success unexpected in common hours.

~ Henry David Thoreau

Everyone Has a Gift

In America today, most people are unfamiliar with the idea that every person has one gift. You can think about this elusive concept however it rings true for you, perhaps simply as your "one gift." Throughout history, people of different traditions have discovered this as true, giving "it" different names:

- In Hindu tradition **DHARMA** is described as the essential quality of a person.

- In the Hebrew tradition, a person's soul or spirit is called **NESHAMA.**

- In ancient Egyptian mythology, a person's **KA** was his expression of life's vital energy.

- The Chinese call this very same energy **CH'I.**

Billions of people are walking around the planet. Why should all of these people know their unique gift, and why is this so valuable and critically important? You've heard the saying "Knowledge is power." The same holds true for *self*-knowledge and your gift. Your gift is a key component of all the information that makes you who you are. Self-knowledge is power! **Knowing your gift** along with other information about your true nature **empowers you to apply this knowledge to the choices you make in your career and life,** setting yourself up for an engaged life and success.

> *Everybody is a genius. But if you judge a fish by its ability to climb a tree, it will spend it's whole life thinking it's stupid.*
>
> ~ Albert Einstein

On the other hand, **without this self-knowledge you are powerless to make choices in your life that reflect and allow you to express who you truly are.** This lack of a sense of intention can make the greatest difference. Without a fundamental understanding of who you are, you risk not making the right choices. In fact, you could make very *poor* choices—choices which cause you to feel dejected because they are not in line with key parts of your nature.

The process of discovering your one true zone identifies your personal gift. Your gift is the natural expression of what you give to the world; it is the inherent talent with which you were born. To discover it, to know it, can change everything for you.

Your True Greatness

Author and psychotherapist Stephen Cope eloquently speaks about this process in his book *The Great Work of Your Life: A Guide for the Journey to Your True Calling,* published in 2012. He describes our one true zone as our internal fingerprint, nothing less than the "subtle interior blueprint of a soul." Cope believes that finding, knowing and using one's one true zone is the exception rather than the rule. If a person believes that we can only be fulfilled by choosing an authentic path—by being who we are, not who others want us to be—and then doesn't follow that genuine path, his energy dissipates. That person survives, but doesn't thrive. His spirit deadens.

******

Your Unique Gift Unleashed

When you recognize your brilliance, your core genius, you will see that **your gift affects all the key areas of your life.** Relationships, work, hobbies, spiritual practices, your family—all these things cannot help but be moved by your offering, even if it is not obvious. It is significant because it is used in so many places in your life that, with awareness and direction, its impact can multiply exponentially.

It is said that we have an obligation to find that force within ourselves and to share it with others. Spiritual leader Deepak Chopra says, "There is one thing you can do and one way of doing it that is better than anyone else on the entire planet."

Your gift is always there and ready to impart itself. It can be a burst of understanding that often comes while interacting with those who have insights of their own. In fact, it can come with such ease that we often take it for granted. And **while your gift never changes, your understanding of it can grow and evolve over time.** This growth of understanding, when applied to your career choice, opens the door to a harmonious, rewarding experience.

Going With the Flow

When your work is effortless, you are in your one true zone, where working rarely feels like work. Your gift is synchronistic with your work. It resonates with you. Work feels spontaneous. The feeling need not be planned. You can make progress with little or no awareness on your part.

This mental state, where deep immersion in a particular activity produces a feeling of instantaneous joy, became known as "flow" because of the work of Hungarian psychology professor Mihaly Csikszentmihalyi. In his work entitled *Flow: The Psychology of Optimal Experience*, Csikszentmihalyi theorized that when an individual is enveloped in the flow state of mind, this energized, concentrated attention to the task at hand unconsciously wipes out an awareness of everything else. The individual happily succumbs to getting lost in whatever he or she is doing.[10]

When you know what your gift—your natural and unique intelligence—is and use it, you feel fulfilled and engaged in your work. You become ready to jump into new situations and implement your gift. When you know what your gift is, you can experience the exhilaration of forward momentum. Your inner thoughts and feelings match your actions, without feelings of conflict or pretense.

What happens, though, when you don't use your gift? Initially you may notice that something doesn't feel right. When you're uncomfortable in your own skin or you feel out of touch or ineffective, then you are not in a place where your gift is naturally operating.

You are the only one who can personally measure or even identify these very subjective feelings. When you use your gift, you go with the direction you are being pulled and feel the effortless progress being made. If you are not using your gift, you have to struggle to make any kind of advancement.

When you follow your instincts, you will see that where

they lead you feels right and natural. When your gift is used regularly, you make the shift from simply getting by, not feeling in sync with yourself, to feeling that "in-the-zone" experience. Once uncovered, your gift is forever linked to what is calling you, tied to your deepest passion, making what you love to do in life better and more rewarding than ever before. It will allow you to create a career you will enjoy and even more importantly a lifestyle you will love.

Your calling is something inside of you, desperately waiting to be released. Without any rational reason to support your belief, you just *know* you were meant to do something, but you don't know *why* or often *what* that something is…you just know. Figuring out your calling is a critical piece of the puzzle. It is what moves you toward creating whatever you want in life, enabling you to get to the place where "work is play." This is the natural channel of our creative energy.

To uncover and discover your calling—to feel the exhilaration of that "aha moment" in your life—is truly wondrous! Maybe you have heard about this but have yet to experience it. If so, you need to pay attention to the feelings you have during "quality" moments in your life.

When college students and graduates recognize their unique gift and become aware of other key elements representing who they are, they are empowered to make choices in their careers and lives that allow them to do what they do and love naturally. They are able to express themselves as who they truly are, giving them the best chance to live engaged and satisfying lives. At the same time, they will create value that is both emotionally and financially rewarding.

Your calling is the way to express your unique gift, your genius. Your life up to now has been leading to this. It is your expression of your gift to the world—something that only you can offer:

- It is a part of who you are.

- It is a higher calling to serve humanity.

- It is an expansion and an evolution of who you are.

There are many different ways you can view your calling. You may see it as...

- a mission only you can accomplish.

- your reason for being.

- your reason for getting out of bed in the morning.

In his interview with Adam Bryant of *The New York Times,* James P. Hackett, president and chief executive of Steelcase, based in Grand Rapids, Michigan, talked about meeting Bill Marriott:

> I remember being struck by the look in his eyes...that he knew who he was. I wanted to have that quality as a leader, where it's really clear who you are and what you stand for. It's about being authentic....Since then, I've met just about every CEO who runs a big company. The ones I'm most impressed with do not seem packaged. They have this sense of peace, this self-awareness that says, "I understand who I am."[11]

Self-Knowledge: The First Step Toward a Meaningful and Rewarding Life

Discovering your one true zone is about the marriage of financial success and a rewarding life. These things can and should go together, each one lifting the other in mutual support. The first step toward creating this life is gaining critical self-knowledge. This begins with knowing your unique gift so that you (or your daughters or sons) are empowered to make choices that are aligned with this knowledge.

Self-knowledge is power. Giving young adults the opportunity to gain this knowledge enables them to embrace their greatest potential in all facets of their lives. Imagine what an incredible difference discovering their gift and true nature can make. It would deliver to their doorstep the opportunity to express themselves fully and to participate completely in the world. Imagine the enormous potential for them to be successful, as well as to make a meaningful contribution to the world, having tapped into their exclusive way of participating.

Imagine, too, the difference it would make if this self-knowledge were cultivated early on. Students would start by making a **focused, informed choice for a school** that is good for them. Instead of having a "five- or six-year party," what if they utilized their four years of college to gather this self-knowledge and test it through real world experiences? **By the time they graduated, they would already be empowered to make choices aligned with who they are.** Imagine the kind of contribution our young people could make. The positive possibilities are endless!

The Rewards of Going
into the Interview with
Self-Knowledge:
Clarity, Confidence & Getting the Job

When you recognize your gift, you gain something intrinsic that cannot be taken away. Once you discover this inimitable process for yourself, no one can tell you, "This is not your experience, this is not the way you process the world."

Students gain this self-knowledge by studying themselves inside and out. **They can give concrete examples of how they have used their gift throughout their life without preparation, without hesitation.** This is the quality end result of truly knowing who you really are.

For example, say a college senior is interviewing for his first job and has all of this knowledge about himself and how it applies to possible careers. Surely he will discuss this in the interview. Now let's say that the interviewer challenges any part of this. Suppose he says to this college senior, "Give me an example of when you demonstrated this strength or this quality."

Easy! This student is so self-studied, so prepared, that he can give several examples of when he used his gift, engaged in his passions, or demonstrated certain qualities. The interviewer can't mistake it. It is true, from his heart, communicated by his demeanor and confidence as well as by his words.

Kevin Liles, founder and CEO. of KWL Enterprises, a talent management and brand-development firm, shared a personal story during an interview with Adam Bryant of *The New York Times*. His story illustrates why it is so important to have clarity and confidence on your side:

> I wanted to be the host of a new hip-hop show but I didn't get the job. I was the biggest guy in the marketplace. Given what I'd done, that should have sold me. But I didn't sell *myself*. So, after that, I realized that no matter what I have done before, I had to learn the art of selling. **I had to learn the art of explaining my value proposition...defining how I differentiated myself from everyone else.**[12]

Knowing these components of self is the key to being able to advocate for yourself, to anyone, anywhere and get the job. Students who know their gift and all of the additional key pieces of information will tell you that they "interview" the interviewer to see if the alignment they are seeking is actually present in each potential employment opportunity. This is a huge advantage!

This is the kind of empowerment our children need to be able to get the job and build the foundation for a successful and satisfying life in any economy. With proper guidance and direction, the remarkable possibilities for putting an individual's unique gift to work against a backdrop of clarity and confidence can flourish as never before, one student at a time.

KEY POINTS

1. *Your gift is the distinctive lens through which you see the world, your personal framework for processing everything in your experience.*

2. *When you recognize your brilliance, your core genius, you will see that your gift affects all the key areas of your life.*

3. *When you recognize your gift, you gain something intrinsic that cannot be taken away.*

4. *Self-knowledge is power that enables us to embrace our greatest potential in all facets of our lives.*

CHAPTER THREE

Exploring the Mindset for Career Exploration

> *In order to do a good job a person must like what he or she is doing....Love thy work and you will be successful...If you do things just because you have to, then you will never enjoy work. Nor will you do a good job if you do it simply out of a sense of duty. Stress is often a by-product of such passive or negative attitudes toward work. Paradoxically as it may sound, love of work can be the best medicine for workaholism.*
>
> ~ Konosuke Matsushita

Brandon graduated from college and got an accounting job. Two years into the job, as he was studying for his CPA exam, he began thinking about why he was taking the test and spending so much time studying for it. This led him to reconsider what his career goals were. He was doing fine, but he sensed that accounting was really not for him. Try as he might, he couldn't see himself in his boss's job years down the road.

Brandon decided to try to uncover his one true zone to acquire more clarity about his career. It was suggested that he reach out to people who knew him well to get their take on his best skills that could apply in a job setting. Since people we work with often notice qualities that we ourselves fail to notice, these insights can be key in identifying the right work.

Brandon e-mailed his college advisor. A few days later, the advisor wrote back with a thoughtful note outlining Brandon's key qualities she had always noticed. For example, she said that she thought his number one strength was communication. She also said that he was trusting, had a calm nature, and was able to see situations from multiple perspectives.

But it was the way his advisor started her e-mail that really caught Brandon's attention: "First off, I want you to know it is totally normal to question who you are and what you want to do," she wrote. "I think high schools and colleges fail students by not helping them explore their potential future jobs that may or may not be in line with their passions." She acknowledged the disconnect that exists in college that denies a student's crucial need to develop a clear understanding about the work they are supposed to do once they graduate.

Unfortunately, **few professors and college advisors accept responsibility for helping students with** the dilemma they face upon graduation—the question of which job to take and **how to start their lives in the real world.** Imagine if someone had given Brandon this insight *before* he started his accounting job—while he was still exploring different career possibilities. Wouldn't it have been better to get this information before spending four years majoring in accounting and two years in a job he didn't enjoy?

What gets in the way of our young adults having more self-knowledge and direction in their career goals after graduation? Many challenges facing our students in high school and in college prevent them from having greater lucidity about their best career choices, how to get on the career path uniquely meant for them, and how to sell themselves to get the job. Let's take a look at these challenges.

Challenge #1: Students may get some pieces of self-knowledge in college, but not the BIG picture.

When we look at the field of career exploration, there are a ton of resources available to help consider different career options. Students take personality assessments to determine careers that suit them. They read books and articles about "finding your passion." Often they meet with career counselors and learn about networking and informational interviewing.

So, why do the resources currently available to help students gain an insight into their career options fail to earn a passing grade for so many graduates? Why do so many of them continue to graduate from college without a clue when it comes to the kind of work they should pursue. Why do they continue to land in jobs that are not personally satisfying?

One reason is that tests and resources, while individually valuable, are only pieces of the bigger puzzle. For example, a personality test may reveal your passions, skills or interests. It may also show whether you are an introvert or an extrovert. This information can help you make a good decision when factored in with other key information. By itself, however, it leaves unanswered the question of what work is best for you. **These tests provide relevant and important components of self-knowledge, but they are *just components*.**

Not only are students getting an incomplete picture of who they are from these tests, **the real problem is that they don't know what other key information they are missing.** Also, too often they lack the deeper support or guidance necessary for applying the knowledge they do have to different career paths.

Traditional steps like personality tests ask and try to answer good questions, but not necessarily in the right order. Also, by not including *all* the right questions, the student is denied the opportunity to examine all of the career-puzzle pieces to make an informed and personal decision about their future. We need to give our young adults much more support and ***individualized guidance*** in leveraging all of these great resources so that they will be empowered to apply this knowledge to finding the right work.

Independent strategic consultant Lisa Summers discusses this problem head on. "Education at the college level, maybe even at the high-school level, is missing key teachings because we are giving students skills to 'get a job, and a good one,' instead of finding out what is special about them as a person and then really supporting, teaching, encouraging them to use the educational tools to foster those qualities.

"When that kid can be the best he can be at what works best for him, then everybody wins. The student, the family and society are enhanced. If society and education can create smart kids, though, why are so many people miserable in their work and in their lives?

"It is because the great majority do not love what they do, or even *like* what they do. Careers are so often not related to their specialness, the unique talents, natural abilities and passion of people.

"Many kids feel like failures because no one has ever expressed that there is anything uniquely special about them. This is where we must do a better job. **We need to isolate the specialness that every child possesses;** only then, when these special qualities are uncovered, will things **change dramatically in their favor."**

Challenge #2: College students have access to many professionals, but there is no single professional dedicated to overseeing a student's development from college to career.

Just as they have access to career tests and other resources for "getting clear," students have opportunities to interact with a wide array of professionals and experts who are relevant to their career decisions. There are incredible, dedicated professionals who take interest in our children as they progress through high school and college, and these relationships can be significant and meaningful.

In high school, guidance counselors help students identify colleges that are a good fit, while SAT and essay coaches help improve students' chances of admission to the school of their choice.

Once in college, students can meet with advisors who help them decide on a major. They can meet with their professors and discuss various issues with them. Career counselors can guide them toward finding internships, networking and getting a job after college.

The problem with this is that, while each of these professionals takes responsibility for a specific leg of the journey from high school to college to career, no *one* professional is taking responsibility for guiding the student toward identifying meaningful work. The high-school guidance counselor helps the student get into college but doesn't explain to the student how to take advantage of the experience toward having career clarity. In college, the career counselor helps the student get the job through networking and résumé tips but seldom engages the student in the deep work of discovering the work that is truly most suitable.

These are generalizations, of course, but the problem they point out is unmistakably real. **There is no one professional dedicated to overseeing the whole arch of a student's academic career,** from meaningful self-exploration and information gathering, to the real-world testing of these results through networking, internships and informational interviewing.

While the support and guidance of these wonderful individuals may help a resourceful and engaged student get into college, grasp difficult concepts, choose an interesting major, improve his or her résumé and reach many other milestones in his or her academic career, at the end of four years of college, this same student may still be in the dark about how to apply this education to a career choice in the real world in which we live. At this early time in the student's personal development, the personal "third eye" is of incredible value, yet missing.

Parents as well as kids need to take responsibility for making sure that college is a time for exploration and growth. They must ensure that young adults are empowered to use ALL of the resources available to them to get a clearer picture about their future career choice options and how to navigate the changing career landscape.

Challenge #3: Many students and parents do not approach college as an opportunity to gain clarity.

Many times students do not approach college in a way that supports using the experience toward being prepared in the real world. Starting in high school and earlier, parents make clear to their kids the importance of getting into a good school. The underlying thinking is that as long as they get into a good school, they'll be "fine," meaning that that they'll get a good job and will "figure out" the work they are meant to do.

The problem is that going to college alone is hardly a guarantee for finding a well-paying job or for having clarity about career paths. We need to make sure our kids know that one important purpose of college, among other functions, is to **help clarify their unique role** in the real world, so that four years later they can be significantly clearer about the career path that is right for them.

Intentionality: Acting with Purpose

Instead of thinking about college as an end goal or a final destination, students need to be encouraged to **think about college as the beginning of four years of intentional engagement leading to clarification of the role they want to play in the real world.** This simple shift in approach significantly increases the value and opportunity of college!

The student who approaches college with intentionality gains greater benefit from taking classes and having internships. By listening with intention, as opposed to just listening, the student's potential for deriving meaning and value from the these experiences increases. It is more likely, therefore, that they will lead to suitable potential career paths.

One way to think about the significance of the way we approach college is the analogy of approaching a library. If you go into a library without looking for a specific book, then you may stumble upon a great book or you may not. But if you go into a library knowing that there is a book in there that will make you a millionaire, then you view the library in a completely different way. Your energy and sense of urgency increase. You are driven to locate the book and have a higher chance of finding it.

The way many students approach college now is analogous to going into a library without looking for a specific book. The point isn't that students shouldn't spend some time perusing the shelves. The point is that part of their time should involve an **intention or a goal toward getting clearer about themselves** and the career choice they will face after graduation.

Challenge #4: Many students lack the tools to make the most of college toward identifying meaningful work.

This final challenge is extremely significant. Even if a majority of students have the intentionality and view college as an opportunity to further the clarity they have about themselves and their careers, **many students simply don't have the tools to take advantage of the resources available to them.**

We saw this in the example of Brandon, who e-mailed his advisor two years into a job to try to get some clarity. No one told Brandon while he was still in college that this may have been a helpful exercise toward making the career choice he was undoubtedly going to face after college. If Brandon had been properly prepared before he graduated, he might not have landed in the predicament he now finds himself: being in a career that he does not enjoy. Maybe he could have started out on a more aligned path earlier.

Knowing that college is an opportunity to get clearer about career paths, students need to be empowered to take the right steps to make the most of their experience. The result of these challenges is that lacking self-knowledge about who they are, many students are **unable to sell themselves** and get the job. They ultimately find themselves committed to a career that makes them miserable. This is why it is critically important for students to determine their one true zone—to address all of the challenges they face today and to help give them the clarity and confidence they need to get the job and find meaningful work.

The need for most young adults to go to college to prepare for entering the workforce is even more important for today's students than it was for their parents and grandparents. Yet colleges have not changed since Mom, Dad or Grandpa went to college. Colleges are institutes of higher learning, not career counselors. Colleges educate students as they always have, in their chosen course of study. It has never been their role to decide what that course of study should be or if it is the best choice for the student. Neither are most teaching to address the rapidly changing world. The need to do things differently is greater now than even five or ten years ago!

Maybe someday colleges will change the way they operate. For the time being, however, students need more support, more guidance and more information so they can make prudent choices regarding college coursework and how those choices relate to who they authentically are and to their future career paths.

******

KEY POINTS

1. Students may get some of the pieces of self-knowledge while in college, but not the BIG picture.

2. Many students and parents are not approaching college as an opportunity to gain clarity.

3. Many students simply lack the tools to really make the most of college in identifying meaningful work.

4. Colleges need to change their approach so that students gain personal clarity they can apply to the ever-changing world!

CHAPTER FOUR

Too Little Too Late: The Risks of Not Planning

> Failing to plan is planning to fail.
>
> ~ Winston Churchill

As soon as a toddler is able to speak, well-meaning adult family members and friends begin asking, "What do you want to be when you grow up?" Typical responses from a young child might be a fireman, a doctor, a baseball player or whatever job mommy or daddy does. The question becomes more daunting, though, as children mature and there is a need to answer that question with a plan of action that has lifelong consequences.

The question "What do you want to be when you grow up?" essentially asks, "How do you want to spend a significant part of you adult life?" For a lucky few the answer comes with confidence and enthusiasm. These young people have had an experience at some point in their lives that has helped them to recognize both what they are good at *and* what they love to do. Unfortunately, for most students the answer to that question is elusive or misguided because they did not have a clearly defined process for figuring out how to choose a major and a career path that is fulfilling and productive.

When parents and students are questioned regarding the process they went through in making this monumental decision, they typically give one of five responses:

- My parents thought I should do X.

- I heard about it or read about it, and it sounded interesting.

- I had to make a decision, so I made a choice based on a subject I liked in school.

- Somebody told me it was a great career, one where there were jobs.

- My dad/mom/cousin/friend/neighbor is a ___, and I thought it seemed like a good field.

Sadly, this is the status quo. This is how most people make one of the most important decisions in their lives. However, **we must question the wisdom of this totally random process because most people do not like, let alone *love,* what they do for a living.**

A Narrow World View

Most children grow up with a very narrow view of the world. They observe their parents doing whatever they're employed at from a distance and they may be exposed to four or five personal work experiences. Entering college, they are unprepared to really get what they need out of their experience for clarity to negotiate a career path post college. They don't have the experience from high school, of course, to know what will be fulfilling and helpful for them to successfully move forward.

There are thousands of occupations available in our culture. **How can an eighteen- or nineteen-year-old possibly know which of those will be a good fit or how to prepare for them even if they do know? They are being asked to make a decision they are not equipped to make.**

Think of it this way: Imagine you are on a trip and suddenly the flight attendant comes back and says, "You'll need to fly the plane now." You go up to the front, sit down in the cockpit and look at all the possible buttons to push. Of course, you have no idea what to do. That's the same type of situation an eighteen-year-old confronts when facing the issue of college.

Surprisingly, most parents and students are not too concerned if upon entering college the student does not yet know his or her career path. They feel there is no need to worry because most colleges offer an "undecided major" option. MSNBC.com reported the following findings: "Eighty percent of college-bound students have yet to choose a major. They are expected to pick schools, apply to and start degree programs without knowing where they want to end up! Fifty percent of those who do declare a major change majors two to three times during their college years."

Ideally, if you have some direction, some awareness of who you are before entering college (or at least earlier in college), you can tailor your college experience to explore subjects and work experiences that are in line with who you are. This gives you a head start so you don't waste time—maybe years—after graduation and possibly through your entire work life.

Late Expectations

Changing majors late in their college careers or numerous times can cause students to fall behind schedule when it comes to completing required courses. The U.S. Department of Education's National Center for Education Statistics claims that only about 40% of students graduate from college in four years. A fifth year could boost the total tuition cost by about 25%. Despite this startling statistic, parents base their financing plan on the expectation that their child will graduate in four years.

So, why are students so indecisive? The reasons are many, but one stands out in particular, and it ties into a bigger problem in our society today: **There is so much pressure on high-school students to beef up their college applications by taking honors and advanced placement classes, being involved in extra-curricular activities and participating in community service.** While these outside experiences have obvious value and can open eyes, young adults are not encouraged to slow down and really get to know who they are or how these experiences may fit them. Self-exploration seems to be trumped by their need to get into a good college so that they will eventually be guaranteed a lucrative job.

Some students continue the fast pace by overloading themselves with two and sometimes three majors because they feel that's the only way to stay ahead of the competition. Or they can't settle on a major because they have no real idea what they are really interested in or passionate about. This unfortunate circumstance can have terrible repercussions.

"In the end, people should pursue what they're interested in," said Daniel H. Pink, author of *Drive: The Surprising Truth About What Motivates Us.* "Looking at lists of careers with the highest salaries tends to be a fool's game. It's very hard to game the system, in the sense that situations and conditions change so quickly that a field that is hot today might be only lukewarm in five or ten years," he said. "It might even be non-existent.

"Let's say you see that accountants are getting decent salaries directly out of college, but you don't really like accounting. Chances are you're not going to be very good at accounting and your salary will reflect that. Generally, people flourish when they're doing something they like and what they're good at."[13]

Nicholas Lore, founder of the Rockport Institute, a career coaching firm, and author of *The Pathfinder,* offers his own take on the subject: "Many people equate success with a high income, but how can someone say they're successful if they're not happy doing their work? To me, that's not success."[14]

The whole college process has become less about the journey and more about the end product. This may not be a problem when a student is confident about what the end result should be. However, it is cause for concern when a student is unsure what the end product should be but is, nevertheless, trapped on this frantic, undirected, expensive journey that we call college.

Is it any wonder then why so many people are disengaged in their jobs? This is unfortunate, but—as was said before—it happens because students primarily focus on how they can eventually make the most money, regardless of how much they may like or love what they will do.

There is a clear method to determine what college students will attend. There are even college planners students can turn to for help. Students can learn a great deal about the colleges ahead of time either by conducting research online or by visiting the colleges and seeing first-hand what the school atmosphere is like, the curriculum options, the people, and so on.

There is also a relatively systematic approach to finding work once a student chooses exactly what he or she wants to do. Colleges have career-counseling centers with numerous resources that show students how to write a résumé and a cover letter, what to say and what not to say during an interview, where and when to send résumés, how and when to follow up, etcetera.

Even using these methods, however, the key planning component of deep personal exploration is missing. There is no clear method to help students discover what they love to do and are meant to do so that work will be enjoyable and fulfilling as well as financially rewarding. This gap needs to be filled.

Choosing a Career Path

My paternal grandmother, Mrs. Annie Henderson, gave me advice that I have used for sixty-five years. She said, "If the world puts you on a road you do not like, if you look ahead and do not want that destination which is being offered and you look behind and you do not want to return to your place of departure, step off the road. Build yourself a brand-new path."

~Maya Angelou

The process students go through in deciding on a career choice is significantly deficient. Choosing one's career is one of the most important decisions a person makes; however, the thought and preparation put in by most students pales compared to other major decisions we all make. For instance, think about the process most of us go through when we want to buy a car. We research different makes and models, talk to friends, visit showrooms and test drive many cars before we make our final choice. Imagine how confident students would feel about their career choices if they went through a similar process before picking a major in college and ultimately a career path.

Several recent surveys have concluded that too many adults are not happy in their careers. **A majority of the respondents** described arriving at their jobs and careers circumstantially, without having engaged in self-reflection, career exploration or planning. Furthermore, they **reported being dissatisfied in their careers and regretting that they didn't take the time to "figure it out" earlier.**

These results underscore the **importance and need to undergo the process for knowing yourself early so that you can set goals and have control over your own career** without allowing for arbitrary circumstances or external considerations, such as prestige, money, or parental approval to determine your fate.

Following are some of the responses given by participants in our own survey when asked how they arrived at their career choice:

- My mother or father is an X.

- My mother and/or father thought it would be a good for me.

- I wasn't sure what to do, and most people were doing X.

- I knew X work would be more comfortable.

- I just looked at who came onto campus and signed up for interviews.

- I wanted a structured company with a training program.

- I wanted X location.

- I felt I should do something related to X because it was credible and would give me more gravitas. I never explored how I really felt about it or whether I would like it.

- I was trying to leave my boyfriend. [relocated without researching career choice]

- Coming out of college, I didn't have the training to go right into my top career choice and, based on my personality, it seemed like a good fit.

71

- I just picked my career and course of study [pre-med] because I wanted to make a lot of money and it looked like it would be fun based on the "Doctor" TV shows.

- Initially I just followed what I seemed to be good at relative to other things.

Many of the people interviewed cited the influence of one or both parents. They expressed regret at not having had the opportunity to self-reflect, to set their own goals and to forge their own path outside the wishes and concerns of their parents.

* * * * * *

Young adults really need to choose their own paths, without undue parental influence. Except as noted, these individuals who chose their careers based on the influence of a parent regretted it:

- My father was a court reporter. He had a romantic vision of what a lawyer was and that impacted my thinking.

- My father was extremely successful in X [owning a huge national business], and his viewpoint mattered.

- I always thought it would be great to tell my parents I would be a doctor, and they were supportive.

- My family member [mother's husband] always came home smiling doing career X, so I got a job in career X. [This person is happy in his career.]

People Who Are Successful at Their Jobs Are Self-Aware

Take the time to invest in knowing yourself. **Set goals based on that self-knowledge and use those goals early on as your North Star.** Ignore this crucial step in your development at your own risk!

Travis Bradberry, author of *The Personality Code,* conducted a six-year international study involving 500,000 participants. He tested for self-awareness and cross-referenced those scores with job-performance ratings. More than eighty-percent of top performers scored high on the self-awareness test, while just two-percent of poor performers did. **When students engage themselves in a quest to gain clarity and confidence early on, they dramatically increase their chances for a satisfying and fulfilling career.**

A majority of our interviewees reported receiving no guidance in how to choose a career, having a lack of self-awareness about their interests, passions and even strengths. They reported establishing and navigating their careers with little planning and a lack of confidence. They regretted not having had awareness that would have led them to a more fulfilling career.

* * * * * *

Here's what some of the interviewees who plowed forward without self-awareness had to say:

- I had no guidance. I just figured it out on my own.

- There was little self-reflection in the process of establishing my career. No one ever asked me what my strengths were, and I wasn't aware of them. Even now it seems not to be so clear.

- I have been job hopping; even today I am job hopping. Do I have a "career"? I never had a "plan." I just had the experience from each job I had, which began to formulate an idea of who I am. It has taken twenty years of careers instead of any target goal or plan. I wish I had had the insight, clarity and a plan at the beginning.

- I started college before I was emotionally ready or focused. I wasn't ready to go to college because I had no goals and was not good at goal setting. Looking back, I think goal setting is the key to success. As an adult in my forties now, I think I needed to find a clear reason for school and an idea of where I wanted to be in the future. I regret just wandering aimlessly. I had no clue.

- I find the work interesting, but the stress and pressure of my career makes it much less gratifying. This is not something that I ever really explored or understood ahead of time.

- I just didn't see this for myself. I needed to do the work to figure it out and know myself better. [This person expressed regret at not having started his own business.]

- One interviewee characterized the impact of parents as "pushing" certain career paths, as opposed to giving guidance or supporting and encouraging self-reflection.

Hindsight Is 20/20

To be prepared is half the victory.

~ Miguel De Cervantes

Sources of discontent and unhappiness in people's careers do not evaporate with time or experience. As one interviewee explained, "My biggest disappointment has been that it [the stress and pressure] hasn't gotten easier as I expected it would as the years went on and as I gained more experience." The stress and pressure in her career was not a feature of her work that she had explored or understood ahead of time.

Many expressed the view that a **degree alone neither prepares you for the real world nor helps you figure out your passion, or calling.** One woman described how she learned how to succeed in the workplace. She started at a small firm with no training programs or mentors and had to figure it all out herself. She expressed the view that she would have greatly benefitted from support, direction and clarity. "Graduating doesn't prepare you for work or the real world. The degree doesn't make you qualified. School is just an introduction," she noted. "Right now I have a degree from both Brown and Yale. I'm very disappointed that I haven't done more with my education." She went on to say, "I think my kids assume that they will go to college and things will work out."

Individuals who reported being unhappy in their careers attributed their lack of action and initiative to minimal self-exploration and low confidence. They never searched for "an authentic fit" and expressed a sense of feeling "trapped" in their careers:

- I was overwhelmed by responsibilities in my current job and couldn't imagine pursuing a different path at the same time. I was paralyzed with fear.

- I wouldn't know what else to do. I don't have a huge, overwhelming passion. Inertia set in and that is where I am now.

- I have had a lack of confidence to leave positions sooner and move toward something aligned with my interests.

- Leaving would risk not having a safety net—a place to work where I am surrounded by people I like and respect.

- I stayed out of habit. I felt trapped in a role I didn't like.

- I took the safe routes because of the lack of confidence that I could do more. I had no support or understanding of what made me special, how I stood out in the world.

Self-knowledge is power. **Without self-knowledge and awareness, individuals have little chance to assert themselves in their careers and get out of situations that make them unhappy.** Learning as much as they can about themselves gives young people clarity and confidence early on so that they are empowered to assert their own strengths, passions and gifts in the world.

Is It Too Late?

Knowing what they know now, **individuals who are unhappy in their careers** place a higher value on feeling satisfied and fulfilled in their careers than they did when they were first starting out. They wish they had paid more attention to this early on.

Janie, a participant in our survey, found that she was unhappy in her career, but she eventually did something about it. "It was rewarding to make a lot of money. I learned how to sell and talk the jargon. At first it was very intimidating, but then I learned it and was getting a lot of business, so I felt like I was being successful at it, and that felt rewarding.

"Then I started thinking about it, and the novelty wore off. I lost motivation. I didn't care anymore and felt it was no longer worthwhile. I got sick of doing the day-to-day parts of my job, so I just did what I needed to do. Finally, I reevaluated what I wanted to do with my life and left."

Although Janie was able to make a change for the better, it may be too late for many people in situations like Janie's to start over. We need to encourage young adults to get to know themselves early on so that they can begin their careers on the right track, as opposed to realizing what satisfies them when they are in the middle or end of their careers and when it is "too late" to make a change.

******

Take the Risk Early

Many interviewees, unhappy in their careers, explained that they figured out what they really wanted to do too late. They believed that it was by then impossible to make a change to a career that was more aligned with their interests and passions. Uniformly, these individuals expressed regret that they hadn't taken "the risk" of identifying and pursuing their "sweet spot" career earlier. Adam and Stephen, two of our interviewees, had typical responses:

"The money I earn makes it impossible to switch gears," Adam said. "I feel trapped, but my obligations to family and to work have me backed into a corner. It also doesn't help that I define myself by the size of my paycheck."

Stephen found himself in a similar predicament. "It takes so much guts and risks to change careers, or I would consider doing it. With the commitment I've made to my family, doing something else really isn't an option for me anymore. I believe I need to stay on this path, no matter the stress, frustration or lack of enjoyment." How sad.

Here's how some other participants responded:

- If I had known what I know now, I would never have selected the career I am trapped in.

- Knowing what I know now about my career, I would have definitely paid more attention to what I liked and what I was good at. If I wasn't finding it, I would have kept searching.

- I know now what satisfies me in a career, but I found out 30 years too late.

- A lot of times I feel trapped because I don't have the luxury to go back to school after all these years because of my responsibilities. Our family relies on my paycheck to pay the mortgage. It would be too big of a gamble now. It would not have been earlier.

- When I sold my business, I felt that I had to go work for someone else because I didn't know what else to do. I had no other passions or clear interests that were translatable, and I didn't have the energy or strong desire at the age of fifty to re-figure it out.

Clearly, it's better to take the risk early, while you can. When you are just starting out, you have no mortgage, no dependents and fewer responsibilities. The time to figure out and explore your passion is *before* you start your career. Doing so gives you the best chance for a fulfilling career and life. Take the risk now, or risk having regrets later about what might have been.

* * * * * *

Knowing about yourself—not just what you're good at, but also what you will enjoy—is a process that requires thoughtful reflection and guidance. **It is not enough to choose a career based on what you're good at without considering what you love, what uniqueness about you will stand the test of time, what serves the world, etcetera.**

Even individuals who reported that they were "satisfied" or "very satisfied" in their careers still expressed some regrets or think about what could have been:

- "I am very satisfied in my career, but that doesn't mean that I never consider what might have been had I made other choices."

- One person gave his job satisfaction an "8 out of 10," but later said if he could do it all over again, he would "try to find a career that was more fulfilling that could still make me a lot of money."

Beth is the president of a large public company. Her situation is a perfect example of why the deep work of self-knowledge and discovery is so critically important. Although generally happy in her career, she often wonders what could have been. "I should have done more to learn about myself. Maybe then I would have considered pursuing a career in acting and entertainment. If there had been more self-exploration, I might have had the courage to put it to the test," she explained. "Back then, though, I couldn't figure out how to make it happen."

Some might think that having a job that one loves is just a pie-in-the-sky, idealistic notion. After all, they might say, the primary purpose of work is to make money. But those who go through the process of achieving self-knowledge and learning about their "one true gift" will find that work can be both financially successful and fulfilling.

What Parents Want
for Their Children

Most **parents want their children to find careers that enable them to be self-sufficient and financially stable.** Therefore, they frequently steer them toward majors that match current job-market opportunities. Although this strategy appears to make sense, especially in a tenuous economy, it often backfires when the student loses interest in the course work or when job opportunities change.

The struggle to adapt to this **rapidly evolving environment** is also problematic for traditional universities, where textbooks and instructors often lag too far behind the curve to be of value to the student. Kunal Mehta is a Ph.D. student in bioengineering at Stanford University. He notes that his field is so new and is changing so rapidly that it is difficult to know what to learn. "We have advisors that we work with, but a lot of times they don't know any better than we do what's going to happen in the future."

The key to surviving and thriving in this constantly evolving setting is to know yourself so well that your natural abilities allow you to adapt more easily as things change in the world. It is important to find a career path that is marketable and has the potential for significant earnings; however, experience has shown that when you choose a path you feel great about—one that aligns with your interests, your natural abilities and your passions—there is an even greater potential for higher earnings and job satisfaction.

81

Most parents have faith in the traditional process and anticipate that their child will be adequately supported by their high school and/or college programs and, therefore, will be prepared to make decisions regarding their career choice. Many parents are unaware that there are programs designed to determine their child's interests, natural abilities passions—their "one true zone." Others may be reluctant to invest in these programs. Additionally, over-scheduled students are reluctant to take time out of their already packed schedules to discover something they feel they may already know.

One student interviewed offered this observation: "I find that many of my friends and the people in my classes chose majors out of nowhere. When asked about why they chose their major and what they love about it, most times they seem to panic a little bit and can't answer the question. I understand that many people are still in the decision-making process of what they want to do with their lives, but **I often find that most people make big, life decisions, like the choice of a major, on a whim."**

Students and parents are all too aware of the financial cost associated with indecisiveness about college majors and the fact that so many students are making hasty or uninformed decisions about their career choice. Although it is not the only cause, changing majors—often several times—is one of the major reasons college years are extended beyond the traditional four years. Much money and time is needlessly being wasted. Because colleges usually require students to choose a major by the end of sophomore year, the value of starting school more self-informed cannot be overstated.

Sound Advice

In her article titled "A Letter of Advice to College Freshmen," Erin Falconer, editor-in-chief of the popular website PicktheBrain.com, offered this advice: "It might not seem like it, but **the choices you make now affect the rest of your life.** We'll all be working for a long time; having a job you love is essential to happiness.

"Think about it. People spend more time at work than anywhere else. Do you want to spend your life bored and indifferent, counting the minutes until the end of the day? Right now is the best time to find your passion. You have the free time and resources at your disposal."[15]

We all impact the people around us. We can either inspire those around us or we can bring them down. We can teach the people we come in contact with and share our pearls of wisdom or joy, or we can criticize others and the world around us, radiating toxic energy to those who communicate with us.

The world could be a much better place for all of us if everyone had a career where they do what they love and love what they do. Imagine if you could surround yourself with spirited, content, fulfilled individuals who were making a contribution to the world doing work they loved—individuals who truly loved the forty plus hours of their week, who really felt like work was play. And imagine if you were one of those people! That's a world worth creating!

KEY POINTS

1. Fifty percent of those attending college change majors two to three times during their college years.

2. The U.S. Department of Education's National Center for Education Statistics claims that only about 40% of students graduate from college in four years. A fifth year could boost the total tuition cost by 25%.

3. When students engage themselves in a quest to gain clarity and confidence early on, they dramatically increase their chances for a satisfying and fulfilling career.

4. Experience has shown that when we choose a path we feel great about—one that aligns with our interests, our natural abilities and passions—the potential for even greater earnings and job satisfaction exists.

CHAPTER FIVE

An Organized Process

> There is a much better chance that you will make yourself special, specialized, or adaptable—a much better chance that you will bring that something extra—if you do what you love and love what you do.
>
> ~ Thomas Friedman

Some decisions are easier to make than others. They are no-brainers—decisions so obvious that no one in his right mind would dispute them. Other decisions are not so clear cut, but they are just as important. Place your vote, for or against, and you may emerge a much better person for your efforts, or you may be setting yourself up for a life of unfulfilled possibilities and unrelenting regret.

Deciding whether or not participation in a self-discovery program is right for you falls into this latter category. Moving forward in this direction offers the opportunity to gain unrivaled insight into your personal gift and its impact on your education and career decisions. Opting out of participating sends you striking out on your own, hoping for the best.

Resisting change is natural, but sometimes taking a bold step forward brings about a life-altering transformation of monumental proportions. When it's the bottom of the ninth and the bases are loaded with your Education, Career and Financial Security all waiting to score, the decision you make before the pitcher rockets the ball in your direction can lead to a strike out or a potential grand-slam homer out of the park!

First let's look at some of the concerns people unfamiliar with the unique benefits and value of such a program expressed:

- These programs cost money. I'm already spending a fortune.

- He/she just needs to pick a career path that matches available job market opportunities.

- He/she is too young to know what he/she is meant to do or be without first experiencing the world.

- The program represents a huge time commitment.

- He/she must get a high paying job in this world/economy.

- If he/she follows his/her passion, he/she may not make enough money to maintain the lifestyle we now enjoy.

- I'll wait and see if he/she figures it out in four years at college.

- My kid has a good idea of what he/she wants to do. He/She should pick a major that is lucrative for today's future job market.

- College debt is soaring.

- It's all about networking. Kids can cultivate the connections they and their parents have and it will work out.

Now let's examine the responses to those concerns. Let's focus on the benefits of participating in a self-discovery program:

In response to the potential cost, **the program may actual *save* many thousands of dollars.** This is due to the fact that a **majority of students no longer graduate college in four years.** This is partly due to a lack of jobs after college, which reduces the motivation and incentive to get through it. Many students choose several majors to "cover themselves," whether they are interested in those areas or not. Investing in self-discovery will lead to happiness and increase earnings down the road when students are aligned with the right profession. Helping students early on is like the Mastercard commercial says: "Priceless."

The next point, that young adults should choose a career path that matches available job-market opportunities, also presents problems. **Employment trends can completely change by the time a student graduates.** What if the skills they developed in college don't match the changing landscape? And even if they manage to find a job in what is the new "hot area," what if they discover that they don't really like what they are doing? Their options are somewhere between few and none if they didn't prepare for anything else even remotely close to what they may like or naturally excel in.

Now let's consider the idea that students entering college are too young to know what they are meant to do or what they are meant to be without first experiencing the world. It is true they are young and inexperienced and unaware of what is out there in the real world; nevertheless, there are key elements every young person possesses that are with them from a young age. Most important among these elements is their unique gift, their personal brilliance—how they see and operate in the world. **Once they understand this key component of themselves, they will be able to use it to their greatest advantage when choosing majors, college course choices, and career paths**—choices that will impact the rest of their lives!

Most people never realize they have this gift, but once they become aware of this amazing missing element, the "aha moment," or epiphany, is career and life altering. Multiple sources and references prove how this **personal revelation can be extremely beneficial in marketing oneself** in the interview process and in gaining confidence, self-awareness and self-clarity. Later on students can put this knowledge to the test in real-world job markets, where they can determine which direction feels like the right fit for each of them.

What about the time commitment? What about the idea that children are already so busy that they don't want to do more work? There is so much school work during the year that they want to just chill out or make money during the summer or during breaks. It's true that self-discovery represents a personal commitment unlike any other, but taking part in a process to figure out your one true zone is both fun and rewarding. **It's beneficial for youngsters to get the opportunity to slow down and decipher through self-exploration who they are and where they fit in the world.** And it is of great value to do it at this time in their lives.

Now let's consider the need to get a high-paying job. Of course, it is important to find a career path that is marketable or that has the potential to earn good money in today's challenging world, particularly if that is the student's key goal. What we have learned, however, is that **achieving even greater earnings (and satisfaction) is more likely if you are also choosing a path that aligns with your interests, natural abilities and passions.**

Successful people speak about this over and over again: If you love what you do and choose a career path with a potential for high income that also fuels your passion, it is the equivalent of a home run for life. An example is former Yahoo executive Tim Sanders. He opined, "Business people who are the busiest, the happiest, and the most prosperous are the ones who are the most generous with their knowledge and their expertise. People who love what they're doing, who love to learn new things, to meet new people, and to share what and whom they know with others: these are the people who wind up creating the new economic value and, as a result, moving their companies forward."[16]

There are countless ways to make significant money, and if you really connect with what you are doing, you will gladly work hard to find the best ways to excel financially beyond your expectations. The last thing you want is to be trapped in a torturous job that has you desperately counting the seconds to Friday every Monday morning. **Love what you do and work will never feel like work.** (A key to making the "big money"!)

The next concern that parents expressed was that their children will not be able to have as good a lifestyle as they have been able to enjoy. This is natural and is especially true in today's world, where it is much more difficult for graduates just coming out of college to get a job aligned with what they studied. That is why it is critical for young adults to know exactly *why* they will be absolutely great and successful in their chosen career path.

When looking for a job, the **interviewee must be able to communicate this information effectively and enthusiastically** to potential employers. The candidate must be able to stand up to the catch-22 challenge from potential employers: "Come back when you have experience." Of course, it is that very same experience that the interviewee is hoping to gain by being hired by that company. With full immersion in the process of self-discovery, the interviewee can provide distinct details about himself/herself that demonstrate that he/she already has personal life experiences that align with the chosen position.

Marketing yourself with these skills, knowledge and clarity will come more easily if you know for sure what path you want to take, why you want to be on it, and how to communicate this fact effectively over and over. In short, **through this authenticity, you can become an expert in selling yourself in any environment.** Again, that translates to higher and higher earnings! After getting your first opportunity, if you stay true, clear and focused to what you know you will love and excel in, you will be able to utilize these key tools to keep taking it higher and higher.

Many parents have an unspoken hesitation to give their child the truly valuable gift/benefit that comes with the discovery of their one true zone. It is understandable that they are skeptical about whether their child actually needs special guidance. If their child figures everything out early in his/her college career, they may even think they are denying that child the opportunity of a full college experience. Nothing could be further from the truth. Arming your child as early as possible with the self-knowledge realized through participation in a process will ignite his/her passion for experiencing college to extraordinary levels.

Many parents feel that students should pick a major that will lead to a lucrative career as soon as they enter college. They believe that their children have a good idea of what they want to do. Many college students, however, end up being unhappy with their first choice. As mentioned previously, many students change majors two or three times, a practice that extends their time in college beyond four years.

There are several reasons students are unhappy with their original choice of major. Some are influenced by their regard for a favorite teacher. They choose the subject taught by that teacher as their major only to find that concentrating on the subject does not hold their interest. Other students start out by choosing a major they think will please their parents. After taking a few courses in their chosen field, they realize that they are not stimulated by the subject. In both cases, the students switch to another major in hopes that they will find their passion.

Changing majors multiple times wouldn't be so bad if the final choice was the right one for the student. If they link their major with their passion and ultimate right career path, then all could be well. However, statistics have shown for decades that the majority do not.

Another concern was debt. It is true that young people and/or their families are being saddled with thousands of dollars of debt as a result of college and graduate-school costs. However, it only makes matters worse if, after being buried by mountains of debt, the graduate finds he or she does not like the chosen path. That is a sad, unfortunate place to be as a young adult.

Commenting on estimates he has compiled on student debt, Mark Kantrowitz, publisher of *FinAid* and *Fastweb,* stated that in 2010 student-loan debt outpaced credit-card debt for the first time. Kantrowitz fully expected this amount to top a trillion dollars in years to come as more students go to college and more of them borrow money to do so.[17]

The last point regarded networking. Some parents felt that if they just cultivate the connections they and their children have, it will work out well. We agree that **networking is critical!** This is why we believe every young person needs to become a networking expert! In fact, **networking is an integral part of being great at marketing and selling yourself** in any environment.

Simply because their family isn't "connected" does not preclude young adults from creating amazing networking connections of their own. This is a must. Connections they make now will be connections they have for the rest of their lives. Learning how to network well is a critical skill that should be cultivated in any self-exploratory, career-coaching program.

And yes, many people get lucky. They are in the right place at the right time to make the connections that count. While this serves as the basis for success for a number of people, we can never depend on it to happen to us. We have to make our own luck and nurture our success to create a future where anything is possible.

Own Your Zone

When you determine beyond any doubt your own right path, your resilience, your marketability, your level of satisfaction and gratification, and your emotional muscle become much stronger. Add to that the tools to "get the right job" in less time and you have a fighting chance to succeed.

When given the chance to explore various areas and discover a lot about themselves through a deep self-exploration/identification process that reveals their "sweet spot," or true zone, young adults will be much more capable of knowing which path to follow without floundering from one misstep to another. This exposure provides the confidence to eliminate the need to rush through critical decisions, enabling a thoughtful and productive embrace of the future by matching what they are learning to who they are.

Young people can focus on multiple career paths that mesh with their one true zone and create a plan that fuels both a financially rewarding career and personal satisfaction. This direction honors the important role money plays in planning a future while acknowledging that when it comes to intelligent career choices, money isn't everything!

Do not wish to be anything but what you are, and try to be that perfectly.

~ St. Francis De Sales

A person can succeed at almost anything for which they have unlimited enthusiasm.

~ Charles M. Schwab

Pay Now, or Pay Later!

Pay now or pay later. That about sums up what is happening to many people and what will continue to happen if the way we as a society approach our career choices does not change. **Essentially, students can put the time, money and effort into becoming self-aware,** firm in their understanding of what their gift, calling and passions are *before* choosing a career, **or they can pay later after the money has been spent, years have been wasted and they are unhappy in their careers.** Paying later goes well beyond the financial impact when people are stuck in jobs they dislike.

The Rise of Student Debt

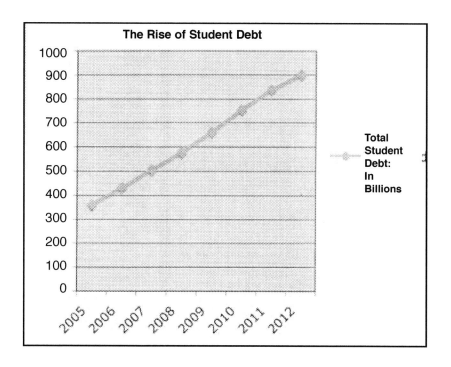

The Rise of Student Debt from 2005–2012: A Report from the Federal
Reserve Bank of New York, Released March 29, 2013

Average Student Debt

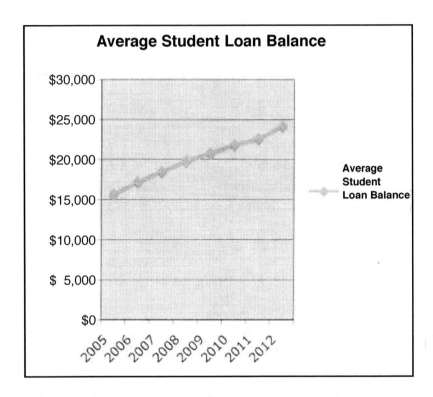

The Average Student Debt from 2005–2012: A Report from the Federal Reserve Bank of New York, Released March 29, 2013

KEY POINTS

1. Resisting change is natural, but, sometimes taking a bold step forward brings about a life-altering transformation of monumental proportions.

2. Employment trends can completely change from the time a student enters college to when he or she graduates.

3. Love what you do and work will never feel like work.

4. Students can put the time, money and effort into becoming self-aware before choosing a career, or they can pay later after the money has been spent, years have been wasted and they are unhappy in their careers.

CHAPTER SIX

On the Sunny Side of the Street

> When love and skill work together, expect a masterpiece.
>
> ~ Charles Reade

With so many of the nation's workforce not engaged in their jobs, what can be said about the remaining 30% or so who love what they're doing? What are their secrets? Where did they find the wisdom and good fortune to pursue careers so perfectly matched to their passions and personality? What made it possible for this happy minority to discover successful careers that were both financially and emotionally rewarding?

These questions and others are revealed through a series of interviews conducted with individuals who steadfastly reject the rule followed by the vast majority, the rule that says you can't make money and be happy, too. The positive, successful people interviewed for this book know this isn't true. These are their stories.

What a Difference a Mentor Makes!

One of the cornerstones of building a successful career is recognizing the importance of mentors. **There is no substitute for having a mentor or mentors on your side.** If you aren't fortunate enough to have found one through school or other avenues, career-coaching programs with individual support and accountability can be extremely helpful in this regard. Additionally, participants in self-discovery programs learn crucial networking and informational interviewing techniques. These skills help students learn how to secure internships which, in turn, can also be an avenue that enables them to find mentors in their field of interest.

Through the personal coaching process, coaches and other mentors get to know you very well. They learn your history and help guide you towards a career path that will lead you to a future of personal satisfaction and success. Most of the wildly successful people interviewed who are happy in their careers were fortunate to have had a mentor. The significance of this finding cannot be overlooked.

It takes one person—just one—to see something special in someone else, to lift her up and give her a chance. My mom used to say, "Everyone needs a cheerleader."

~ Wilma Rudolph

Jeff, Analyst in the Stock Market

Jeff, a very happy, successful, well-known analyst, met his mentor when he was eighteen. His mentor educated him about technical analysis in the stock market. Jeff's interest was fueled by his fascination for watching the tape showing the stock numbers, and by seeing how price/value changes impacted whether you were making or losing money. Jeff's mentor took advantage of this and taught him a way to predict the prices and price formations.

Realizing at an early age that he naturally liked learning about the world from older, more experienced people, Jeff embraced his mentor's lessons and his mentor's wisdom. "Everyone should have someone to guide them, someone who has lived through more than you in the area of your greatest interest/career…who understands more than you do…who can advise you beyond your own understanding, simply because you have not been around as long as they have."

******

Doug, Real-estate Lawyer

In college, Doug majored in finance and accounting under the assumption that he would become an accountant. He never really pushed himself to excel. Once he met Dave, though, all bets were off. The reason? Dave was focused on working hard, going to law school, and becoming a financial success. For Doug , it was a wake-up call.

Dave's profound influence as a mentor to Doug inspired Doug to follow a similar path. He decided to pursue a new interest—law. He planned to combine this interest with his interest in real estate, which he had developed from early exposure to his family's real estate business. Most importantly, he realized that for this new career path to bring him financial success, like Dave, he would have to focus and work hard.

For Doug, setting his sights on a new career path took courage and a tremendous amount of effort. It wasn't easy, but Dave's advice to Doug always gave him the strength to persevere: **"Once you decide what you really want, you need to work hard to achieve it."** This belief mirrors the philosophy behind discovering your one true zone: when you know the right career path for you, working hard to reach that goal will feel like play.

Action is the foundational key to all success.

~ Pablo Picasso

Beth, President of a Large Public Company

Beth's mentor was the professor of a communications class she took in college. From the start, the professor realized that Beth was a "gifted communicator." She asked Beth if she had ever considered going to graduate school for a degree in communications. Beth noted that it doesn't surprise her that it was her professor and not her advisor who was able to see her strength as a strong communicator. A professor, she noted, has the opportunity to observe students in action and get a sense of their strengths, potentials, interests and talents.

Beth considers herself fortunate to have had such an insightful professor take a genuine interest in her. What she regrets, though, was not having any networking opportunities to serve as her entrée into the communications field.

The right career-coaching support/program can ensure that participants have the advantage of mentors who get to know them well and take a vested interest in guiding them along a career path that plays on their singular gift, supports their passion, and fits their personality and goals like a finely tailored suit.

* * * * * *

Hard work becomes easy when your work becomes your play. Never underestimate the value of loving what you do.

~ Timothy Ferriss
Author of *The 4- Hour Workweek*

Steve, Chemist

Steve was a chemistry major whose parents wanted him to attend medical or dental school. Steve, however, felt his passion was actually in chemistry and had hopes of pursuing a Ph.D. in that arena. He took the initiative of seeking the advice of a well-known and well-connected professor in the field. This professor encouraged Steve to pursue his passion and became his mentor. He eventually helped Steve obtain his first position at Merck.

When he was forty-two, Steve obtained a second mentor, one who was instrumental in moving him further along in his career path to working in his own one true zone. This mentor owned a private personal-care company and encouraged Steve to pursue his passion in product development. He subsequently introduced Steve to new technologies, new products and new concepts. He also recognized Steve's innate ability to relate to people and to present technological developments in a way that non-scientists could understand. He asked Steve for help in establishing his company internationally, and together they gained tremendous success in this endeavor.

Steve has no doubt about the important role mentors played in his climb to the top. He offered this advice to individuals starting out in their own careers: "Find a mentor when you are young, someone who cares about you, that is all that matters. Find someone with the knowledge you're seeking, someone who sees you as a whole human being."

Lauren, Owner of a Business Coaching Firm

As a young person, Lauren was continually relied upon by friends to help with issues pertaining to relationships. This pattern became obvious to her at an early age and helped launch Lauren on a path towards her one true zone. Refining this path, however, took the wisdom of a mentor who recognized Lauren's natural gift/ability to look at a whole picture and put the pieces together.

Lauren's mentor was the one who helped her see coaching as a career in which she could marry her interests/talents/gifts with her love of psychology. "Being able to see the big picture, look at it, and fit the parts together to see what needs attention, what is naturally strong in a person" made all the difference in the world to her. Lauren's love of what she is doing and great success in her field have been a natural extension of her own clarity and perspective, buttressed by the early support of a mentor.

* * * * * *

Say yes to any opportunity to do anything even close to what you dream of doing. This will sometimes get you in over your head, but that will just make you swim harder. It's the best way to meet other people who love to do what you love to do. You will learn from and comfort each other.

~ Stephen Colbert

The Importance of Early Recognition of Natural Abilities

Lee, A Writer and Radio News Anchor

As early as high school, Lee began to recognize her natural ability for storytelling. Her special capabilities and qualities included writing and communication skills, empathy, self-expression and expression on behalf of others. She believes this recognition began while analyzing approaches to characters in high-school theater productions.

Lee learned even more about herself through various work experiences in college: coat-check clerk, bellhop, and front-desk clerk. At NYU, Lee did some shifts at the college radio station, where she fell in love with the medium. A self-starter, Lee took advantage of as many internships as she could, and while she does not credit a formal mentor for her success, she was influenced by those she considers masters in their craft.

"I studied their techniques and philosophies. I asked a lot of questions and made it a point to keep my eyes and ears open, especially on the intern level, when I had everything to learn and nothing to lose."

The importance of multiple internships cannot be overlooked. The more opportunities one has to experience "a day in the life of an…," the higher the likelihood that you will find your match. That said, **it can be equally valuable to take part in internships where you learn what does *not* interest or move you.**

Lisa, Actress and Voice Teacher

When she was fourteen, Lisa's natural singing ability caught the attention of someone who recognized her talent. This meeting led to a connection with a famous voice teacher. A short while later, on what was the second audition of her life, she won the lead in a Broadway show.

Lisa realized through that series of events how incredibly lucky she had been. She struggled after that, always coping with the insecurity of trying to repeat her initial success, trying to land a role in another Broadway show. All the while she was constantly looking over her shoulder for someone to come along and take it all away from her.

In short, Lisa couldn't keep up with her own success. What got her back on track was getting into an acting class and working with a voice teacher. She began developing her craft, technique and tools with the attention and intention of a marathon runner, instead of a sprinter. Lisa made a life-long commitment to her career, so that she no longer felt that getting her first Broadway role was a fluke. She built herself from the ground floor up as a person fueled by the talent she worked so hard to develop and nurture. Sure, luck was a factor when it came to auditions, but it no longer held the dominant position, nor was it perceived as a threat to her future endeavors.

Lisa believes that anyone in any career path, if ill-equipped with the tools of the trade, both practical and emotional, will struggle to succeed. Based upon her own experience, she feels kids must know and understand their personal characteristics, their special gifts, in order to excel in whatever career path they choose down the line.

Roger, the Owner of a
Chiropractic Practice and Author

At a young age, Roger realized that he was a leader. People always asked for his advice, and he came to understand that his calling was to be there to help make a difference in their lives. He also realized how much he loves to connect with people and help them smile. By Roger's way of thinking, "There are no problems, just roadblocks which are actually gifts to grow."

David, Senior Vice President and General Manager
at a Major Network

In fifth grade David's teacher pulled him aside and said, "When you do something in class, the class buzzes around and it is hard to keep everyone in line." While the teacher viewed his behavior as a negative and disruptive, David learned over time that his high-energy nature and leadership quality could be a plus if used correctly.

As an adult, David realized that people galvanize around the energy he brings. "I think people like the positive energy, glass-half-full attitude and enthusiasm that I naturally have," he noted. "As a leader and mentor I am able to inspire people to work their best and to be open to finding new ways of doing things. I believe my natural enthusiasm is the connection that enables others to do *their* best work."

Debbie, Teacher

When she was a child, playing "teacher" was always one of Debbie's favorite games and as far back as she can remember she loved teaching her siblings and tutoring her friends. She was especially good at math.

As a young adult, she developed an interest in special education. She combined her skills in math with her deep desire to help people by volunteering to help students suffering from Cerebral Palsy with their math homework.

The concept of making a difference in this world was part of the household Debbie grew up in and internalized. "I was raised by parents who instilled the responsibility to make a difference. We were taught that life is not all about you!"

******

Jay Leno tells about a conversation with Mrs. Hawkes, his high-school English teacher, and how it changed his life:

"I always ... hear you telling stories in the hallway, and people seem to be laughing. Why don't you write those stories down and I'll accept them for class credit?...Have you ever thought about becoming a comedy writer?"

Although I had always been a showoff and a cutup, it never occurred to me that you can make a living by writing comedy, and so the question sort of changed my life....It was a real turning point in my life.

~ Jay Leno

Finding Your True Passion

When you make a decision because you really love what you are doing, because you're really passionate about it...and because you'd do it no matter what the outcome—that's when you become most successful.

~Alicia Keyes

Several surveys have shown that a majority of people do not know their true passion and that they would be happier if they did. Self-knowledge is the key to identifying your true passion. One way to gain this knowledge, in part at least, is to ask yourself several questions:

1. What makes you happy?
2. What makes you feel as though you are contributing to others?
3. What makes you feel creative?
4. What would you do even if you weren't being paid?
5. What are you good at?
6. What comes easy to you?
7. What would you try to do that you have never done?
8. What do you like to discuss with others?
9. Did you ever have an aha! moment? What were you doing?
10. What makes you want to get out of bed in the morning?

Undergoing the process which reveals their one true zone helps young people look for the threads in their lives that can lead to the discovery of one's own gift. Once discovered, this gift should be part of everything you do.

Self-knowledge of one's natural gift is a powerful advantage when interviewing and also in choosing a career path. Think back to David's story. Such self-awareness has certainly worked for him as a key factor in his decision-making process. "I always paid attention to myself and would advise others to do the same. Get to know yourself. Listen to the voice inside. Knowing yourself will help you get what you want."

Your work is going to fill a large part of your life, and the only way to be truly satisfied is to do what you believe is great work. And the only way to do great work is to love what you do. If you haven't found it yet, keep looking. Don't settle.

~ Steve Jobs

KEY POINTS

1. One of the cornerstones of building success-ful careers is recognizing the importance of mentors. There is no substitute for having a mentor or mentors on your side.

2. Early recognition of your gift is important.

3. When you're on the right career path, work-ing hard to reach that goal will feel like play.

4. Your career path should be enriched by your singular gift that supports your passion and fits your personality and goals like a finely tailored suit.

CHAPTER SEVEN

The Foundation of Success

Do what you love and you'll never have to work a day in your life.

~ Confucius, 500 B.C.

The **philosophy expounded in this book is based on the belief that we all have one true gift**—the distinctive lens through which we see the world, our personal framework for processing everything in our experience. It adheres to the **necessity of recognizing your one gift** in terms of your natural abilities, your passions and your calling. You must work with these qualities on your path to a successful career. Self-clarity opens the door to creating the life you want!

112

In the search for our unique gift, both personal strengths and personal weaknesses must be considered: **strengths** because they **serve as a foundation upon which everything else is built**; weaknesses because they provide greater insight into the complementary skills to look for in a partner or team member. Knowing your shortcomings can help build great relationships in your life. It is particularly powerful in running and building your own successful business or practice so that you have a well-rounded organization with all your needs met.

> *To know people is wisdom, but to know yourself is enlightenment. To master people takes force, but to master yourself takes strength*
>
> ~ Lao Tzu

Again, successful people who love what they're doing typically achieved their status by following these same strategies to reach that goal. Here are a few of their stories:

Jeff, Executive at a Mortgage Company

Jeff is currently Chief Administrative Officer, Legal Officer and Secretary for a mortgage company. He oversees legal affairs, management affairs and intellectual property. Jeff recognized as early as middle school that he was able to achieve a good understanding of things very quickly. He considers his ability to master things rapidly his main natural skill, or strength. This is his gift.

"The first time I hear something, I hear it clearly and get into things deeply and very quickly." Jeff explains that he is able to utilize this strength to move from one project to the next ahead of the curve. This talent paved the way to his successful career.

While he has a gift for mastering things very quickly, Jeff is not averse to seeking help from others when necessary. "My own ignorance or naiveté does not keep me from acting. I will try anything. I am not afraid. I see this mostly as a positive. I can see 85% of what is needed to complete a project. Then I figure it out. But I know to get people to do what I cannot do or see."

Sara, Principal of a Preschool

Sara is the principal of a preschool and loves her work. Her parents really encouraged her to follow what she felt good doing. She didn't grow up with a lot of money, and the desire to earn a lot of money was not a contributing factor in her career-making decisions.

Looking back, Sara feels like her career chose her. Teaching makes her so happy. It gives her a sense of fulfillment and makes her feel smart. "I sometimes feel like I'm living a charmed life," she remarks. Sara credits getting where she is to a series of lucky events and to the fact that she found her passion and followed it. She advises young people to "know your needs."

Sara compares her husband's career to hers. She explains that for her husband, work is what allows him to live the rest of his life and enjoy his hobbies and leisure; that is enough for him. For Sara, on the other hand, her work *is* her life. Her work *is* her hobby. She acknowledges that some people are willing to compromise in that regard; she isn't one of them. "I need to sense that what I have is a blessing."

Seth, International Salesperson

Someone told Seth when he was young, "Never lose your enthusiasm." Seth attributes this quality and his optimistic nature to helping him with everything. He currently focuses on global sales for printing of communications platforms.

Seth believes his gift is that of a natural sales closer. He relishes the natural thrill of going inside someone's head and rewiring their brain until they understand that his (Seth's) way of thinking is the correct way. It excites him when a customer becomes enthusiastic about what he is offering them because they evolve into agreeing with his view.

He told us that he possesses a "positive determination not to dwell on the negative." For Seth, it is imperative to "keep moving forward regardless of the chains and weights that may be holding you down. Failure is not an option."

Seth's recognition of his gift enables him to lead a full, satisfying life. "I was born to sell and I am so happy doing it."

Doug, Dentist

Dr. Doug Mahler represents the third generation in a family of dentists. As a child Doug was a good artist and loved working with his hands. He also saw that his father was passionate about dentistry and happy with his career; this observation had a lasting impact on his life. As early as third grade, Doug knew that he wanted to become a dentist and join the family practice. His father encouraged and mentored him to achieve this goal.

Dr. Mahler is naturally a very caring and compassionate person and loves to make his patients feel comfortable. He also excels in his ability to manage people and to multi-task. All these traits were instrumental in his becoming a happy and successful dentist and in his ability to run a thriving practice.

Dr. Mahler also has a "sixth sense" for hiring; he focuses on adding people who have "brilliance" in their own areas of expertise. He enhanced his dental practice by adding professionals who could provide quality support in related areas: periodontist, denture specialist, root-canal specialist, oral surgeon, and others. The office he runs now has twenty-two employees.

While both Doug and his father are excellent dentists, each has different strengths. Their assets complement one another. Doug developed a website for the practice and has been successful in expanding the practice through hiring and also through mergers. His father designed their building with an eye towards creating a warm, calming environment. Their combined qualities resulted in incredible success, as well as a truly great and rewarding partnership.

Larry, TV Journalist and Producer

Currently a corporate consultant and strategist, Larry was also a television journalist and TV news producer, Larry was aware of his passion for news at a young age. That self-knowledge, coupled with the ability to identify his natural strengths and unique gift, launched Larry on a successful career trajectory.

This happened, Larry notes, without the initial benefit of a mentor. "If I had found a mentor earlier in my career, I'm certain I could have been propelled even further." Larry's hindsight observation regarding the importance of having a mentor highlights once again the invaluable role mentors play in career choice and development that can ultimately lead to a well-designed, optimal future, one both personally and financially rewarding.

Larry's success can be attributed to the fact that his career path has been a strong combination of his strengths, gift, and passions. "I always felt wired for this work as a journalist/producer and knew in my heart that this is what I was meant to do."

Larry's career plays to his what he calls his natural strength: resourcefulness. (I call it his gift!) He can creatively think his way out of almost any situation; he is is a natural problem solver! His passion for news and politics, combined with his gift, put Larry in a career that has been his one true zone.

One key element instrumental in Larry's success is his collaborative approach to life. "I'm always desperate to find someone smarter." This self-awareness of when to build a team or partnership to get the job done in the best possible way, with the best possible outcome, ties in with Larry's natural way of operating in the world. It also exemplifies the importance of making networking a natural component of the career-building process.

When personal gifts and passions unite, the end result is nothing short of a miracle come true, where financial security and complete job satisfaction go hand in hand. When the opposite is true, as author and journalist Linda Rowley observed, the end result resonates with negativity. "If someone hates his job, it's doubtful that he'll put a lot of energy into contributing new ideas, increasing sales or productivity, cutting costs or any of the other issues that result in raises and promotions. And he'll probably be the first out the door if the pink slips come."

This is absolutely not the case when an individual is engaged in a career that is right for him/her. In that scenario work really does feel like play. Work really is perceived as fun. The happy, successful individuals interviewed for this book overwhelmingly agree.

Here are some additional highlights from the interviews of people you just read about and others:

Doug said in describing his real estate work, "Our first shopping center grand opening was so much fun. We were given a Lucite door knob and it was one of the greatest gifts I ever received." He recommends, "You must figure out what is fun for YOU!"

Larry advised, "Absolutely find something you enjoy doing. Young people should carve out what they would love to do and then see if it exists. If it does not exist, they will have to create something new and that is totally doable."

Mark observed, "You have to find what you love. You cannot be successful if you don't love what you do. With the time and energy building a career takes, you will not work as hard, or you might give up altogether, if you don't love what you are doing!"

Paul stated, "You want to feel excitement and a sense of accomplishment in your work. The exhilaration of truly loving what you do is a gift beyond measure. I want it for myself. I want it for my children. I never want my kids to come home and be miserable at the end of the day or week of work."

Damon, a successful and skilled attorney, believes that if you love what you do and it fits you, you will find great ways to make money. "Don't go into a career for money," he advised. "Instead, look at what you enjoy and what fits you—that's the way you make money without being miserable. If you follow your passion and link it with your personality—natural talents if you know them—there are so many ways to make money!"

Lee advised, "Look for work that simultaneously stimulates you and gives you a sense of peace. Choose something that you can feel passionate about and be proud of. Challenge yourself. Be conscious of your evolution and never be afraid to take risks."

Roger, a holistic professional, chiropractor and certified instructor for other doctors, has the opportunity to really connect with people. He enjoys this aspect of his career. "What I love most," he says, "is making a difference in the lives of so many people and seeing them smile. That's the best reward of all."

Debbie explained, "I love teaching. I enjoy the diversity, the different projects and being involved with different things. You have to do what you love and then you have to figure out what other avenues you can tie in to nurture that environment."

Julie also has a passion for teaching. She noted, "Teaching and working with children is rewarding and fun. I love knowing that I am making an impact on someone's life. I enjoy watching children grow as learners and people. I love what I do."

People rarely succeed unless they have fun in what they are doing.

~ Dale Carnegie

Always be yourself. It may not be much, but it's all you've got. No one can take that away from you if you don't let them. Trying to be someone you're not takes up too much energy and is no fun.

~ Al Roker

I always told myself that I would leave the minute I was bored and I'm surprised that over all this time it hasn't happened.

~ Sam Waterston (actor)

KEY POINTS

1. People must recognize their passions and natural abilities and work with them on their path to a successful career.

2. Both personal strengths and weaknesses must be considered: strengths because they serve as a foundation upon which everything else is built, and weaknesses because they provide greater insight into the complementary skills to look for in a partner or team member.

3. When an individual is engaged in a career that is right for him or her, work really does feel like play. Work really is perceived as fun.

CHAPTER EIGHT

Racing to the Finish Line

> *My great wish for all of you who have allowed me to honor my calling through this show is that you carry whatever you're supposed to be doing, carry that forward, and don't waste any more time. Start embracing the life that is calling you and use your life to serve the world.*
>
> ~ Oprah Winfrey

Parents universally want what's best for their sons and daughters: the best education, a loving relationship with the partner of their choice, and a life spent immersed in a successful career that is both personally gratifying and financially lucrative. In an examination of how people decide what value to place on projects they've made, research shows that if you feel a sense of creative ownership over something, you irrationally tend to value it at a level more than it is worth. For example, if you build a table to sell at a yard sale, you may value it at $500, whereas people who come to the sale wouldn't pay more than $100 for it.

In a similar manner, **parents often tend to overvalue their children,** seeing them as being more intelligent and more capable than they are. This tendency causes parents to be overly confident about their children's potential for greatness. This is not to say that every child does not have a gift and unique greatness. They do! The reality, though, is that not every child is going to be first in his/her class or excessively successful in life. **By blindly supporting this overvaluation,** especially as it relates to their future, **parents risk failing to take a course of action that would have been in their child's best interest.** Consequently, options and opportunities that could benefit their children are entirely missed.

Young adults need a program and the right coaching and support to help them focus on entering into life with greater intention, clarity, confidence and vision. This **intentionality and meaningful exploration give students an advantage** that they would not have otherwise. Ultimately, this clarity of purpose and intention can change everything by enhancing the college experience and whatever follows. It is truly that valuable.

******

Getting the Most out of College

Some people drink from the fountain of knowledge, others just gargle.

~ Robert Anthony

The term **"curse of knowledge"** was coined by film and TV music composer Robin Hogarth. The basic premise of this principle is that once you know something, it's impossible not to know it, and you begin to assume that everyone knows it. That assumption is not always correct, and when it is not, the "curse of knowledge" makes it difficult to see things from the point of view of others. Curse of knowledge can hinder our ability to communicate our ideas to others. This **comes into play in the education of our children when parents or teachers make the wrong assumptions about what these young adults already know.**

The curse for the educator is that she may see her job as similar to putting a buffet of food in front of the student. From the educator's perspective, it's up to the student and parents as to whether they do something with what is on the menu. Educators need to understand if you set a buffet of information in front of someone who is organized and has the tools and knowledge to take advantage of it, that's a great thing. But a person unfamiliar with the contents of the buffet is totally lost.

Here is how the curse of knowledge may adversely affect a student entering college: He arrives in a collegiate environment that he's never experienced before, led by **teachers and parents who assume he possesses the learning tools to process** all the information and knowledge available to him. This path eventually leads him to a place where he must make decisions about his future—decisions he is not equipped to make. They include getting a job, launching into the real world, and deciding about a career.

The problem for the student is the same one he encountered while in middle school or junior high school and started learning algebra. When he asked why he had to learn the subject, he might have been told, "You learn algebra so you can do calculus, so you can do physics and chemistry, so that you can graduate college and get a job." So, for the seventh grader, the point of doing algebra is for something years in the future.

There are several ways youngsters respond to this explanation: The highly compliant student probably says, "I'll do this algebra."

Many, however, will counter with, "This is stupid. I don't see the point."

In either case, they never really understand what learning algebra is all about, what it's for. A proper response to the seventh grader might have been something like this: "Algebra trains your brain to solve problems. This will help you solve all kinds of problems both now and when you are an adult. Problem-solving skills will help you in your career and in your life."

Discovering your one true zone puts ownership of the educational process inside you. It doesn't concentrate on becoming well rounded, but **focuses** instead **on what you are most capable of succeeding at.** "Own your zone" and it will serve you in countless ways; it is so worthwhile that we have repeated its value throughout this book. Some young adults figure it out by themselves; most don't.

Most graduates leave college with a well-rounded education. They go off and stumble into a first job, then another, which allows them to pay bills. Even if they would like to make a change, they realize at a certain point that they can't stop because they need the money. Before they know it, they've reached middle age wondering "how in the world did I end up doing what I'm doing?" With a little bit of time and a small investment this nightmare can be averted.

When adults perform, they get compensated with money. Children quickly realize that when they perform, they are given an assessment and somehow that's supposed to be their reward. A world that elevates getting good grades above everything else comes at a steep price for children driven to continually excel. These same students figure out, usually around college, that getting straight A's is not enough to provide a full educational experience in the short run and no guarantee of a meaningful, happy and successful life in the long run.

In the film *Race to Nowhere,* which examines the downside of childhoods spent on résumé-building, one student bemoans the fact that everyone expects them to be superheroes. "When success is defined by high grades, test scores, and trophies," a child psychologist says in the film, "we know that we end up with unprepared, disengaged, exhausted and, ultimately, unhealthy kids."

The promise of quality career **coaching and programs** is to

give educational ownership to the student before he/she turns thirty so he/she doesn't hit middle age drowning in a sea of anger and regrets. Hidden opportunities for a better education and a satisfying, financially secure future abound. With the right guidance, these opportunities are available now. Knowing how and where to look, these gems of possibility are yours for the taking.

Going to college and doing well is no guarantee of getting a job and certainly not of having a truly satisfying, rewarding career. The truth is that most of the jobs that exist today will not be what is needed or desired in the future. **Getting the most out of college, being nimble and employable in a changing world and finding meaningful work all start with self-knowledge about who we are and what our true gift is.**

Education begins at home and I applaud the parents who recognize that they, not someone else, must take responsibility to assure that their children are well educated.

~ Ernest Istook

Shifting Gears

As a society, we need to help our children and ourselves shift goals. We have to switch from wanting them to be accepted by the best possible college according to *U.S. News & World Report's* annual list to striving to help them go to college without floundering, with more self-knowledge, more intention, and a greater ability to latch onto the path that aligns with their one true zone.

A paradigm shift is required in our thinking. We need to encourage self-assessment and reflection as a starting point before investing in and making decisions during the college phase. Reflect on the fact that nearly 84% of incoming college freshmen expect to graduate in four years, but the sad reality is that less than half of them will do so. Upwards of 58% of them will take six years to earn their degree. Many others never graduate at all.

With the soaring cost of college and the competitive job market, students benefit from uncovering their one true zone as soon as possible—preferably before entering college. Owning their zone enables them to use their time in college to gain valuable self-knowledge, abilities and experiences. It allows them to become authentic in their journey and to hone their skills and use their gift so they are at a strategic advantage when entering the work force and so they can be happy in their career.

The decision to act is clear—follow the route taken by the many people who are not totally satisfied with their jobs, or take the path less trampled for the education you need, in the time it's supposed to take, to get the career you're supposed to have.

The biggest mistake that you can make is to believe that you are working for somebody else. Job security is gone. The driving force of a career must come from the individual. Remember: Jobs are owned by the company, you own your career!

~ Earl Nightingale

128

KEY POINTS

1. Parents and educators risk assuming students have certain knowledge that they do not have.

2. A buffet of information will only work with someone who is organized and has the tools and knowledge to take advantage of it.

3. While nearly 84% of incoming college freshmen expect to graduate in four years, the sad reality is less than half of them will do so. Upwards of 58% of them taking six years to earn their degree. Many others never graduate at all.

4. We need to encourage self-assessment and reflection as a starting point before investing in and making decisions during the college phase.

5. Learn how to "own your zone."

Afterword
The Genesis of oneTRUEzone

A Personal Journey: Helene Naftali

My own personal journey to find a career that would fulfill me while being financially rewarding was not unlike that of many students. I entered college as a pre-law student with the intent of attending law school upon graduation. After four years, I graduated with a degree in pre-law, but I quickly realized that I had no interest or desire in being a lawyer. I, therefore, left college frustrated and unsure of what my future held.

My experience is not unique. The exorbitant cost associated with college today and the dismal state of our economy contribute to the pressure students feel to select a major and decide on a career path. Many students make that decision, as I did, without a true understanding of what the day-to-day reality of a job entails and even more importantly, without knowing how well suited he or she is for that career. This really bothers me and I am truly committed to changing this for as many young people as possible. Loving what you do is not only possible, it is *critical* for our children's futures.

Like me, students too often commit to a career that's not based on any personal exploration, but on the influence of parents, society, relatives or friends. Students who attend college undecided on a major often feel pressure to make a premature and superficial choice. Some copy the choices of their peers. Others choose a major in which they feel certain to be successful. Still others select a program of study that will please significant others in their lives. There is a better way. I am sure of it.

When we tell adults about oneTRUEzone, an actual process for discovering their gift and calling—what they are meant to do—and for finding a career that can help them lead happy, truly satisfying lives, the typical response is that they wish they knew of this process when they were young. They (and I!) express regret that they did not know about it before devoting so much time, education, energy, and money into a career that was wrong for them. They wished they had had this information before they had responsibilities that come with adulthood and a family.

The development of oneTRUEzone was a thirty-year process for me. As I struggled to find that perfect balanced career for myself—one that would excite me, fulfill me, let me make a difference in people's lives, and make me look forward to going to work every day, I embarked on my own process of self-exploration. In my efforts to discover for myself the work that is my passion (my one true zone), I learned that I have a gift for helping others uncover their own gifts. The result of my own passion, confidence and clarity was the creation of oneTRUEzone, my gift to the young future of our world.

Helene Naftali
Principal and Founder

* * * * * *

131

Anatomy of a Gift and How to Use It

Although I left college knowing I did not want to pursue a career in law, I did not know what I wanted to do. I was fortunate to have an incredibly powerful and moving experience soon after graduation that had a great impact on me and changed my life. This experience led me on a thirty-year journey of reading and learning on a quest to find a better way for myself and others in determining our life's course.

The summer after I graduated Binghamton University, I went with a friend to Europe and Israel. Before leaving, another friend encouraged me to visit and stay with her brother Evan and his wife, Ruth, in Israel. We called them when we arrived. They came and picked us up, and our first day together marked the beginning of a life-changing event for me.

They took us into their home and treated us like family. At their insistence, we stayed there for weeks in their one-room apartment. Although we protested, we slept in their bed, while they slept elsewhere. Ruth cooked all our meals, and they took us everywhere.

What was most amazing was the genuine warmth and personal connection, attention, and love they and each of their ten other relatives gave us the entire time. Today, many years later, they are my closest friends. Their son is my godson. Their family has become mine and vice versa.

I carry this experience with me to this day. I realized then that these were the kinds of relationships and connections I always wanted to have in my life. I was a different person from that day on, and that event signaled the beginning of my desire to connect to others in a way that is just as significant, genuine and meaningful!

A few years after my trip to Israel, I was invited to speak to the graduating senior class at my alma mater, Binghamton University. Totally unexpected, both of these life experiences overwhelmed and enlightened me. They left me with a burning passion to make a difference in the lives of college students. I was "in my zone."

Yet my journey to find my own special gift took me many years and cost me a significant amount of money. When I realized that I was not really happy in my chosen career, I went back to school to become a therapist and spent some time in that field. At the time family and financial obligations prevented me from working as a therapist full time. The experience, however, was a crucial component in enabling me to uncover my true gift.

My "aha moment" came when I experienced the elated feeling I had when given the opportunity to speak to the graduating class at Binghamton. That is when I finally found my own special one gift—the gift for helping others uncover their own gifts. This gift, coupled with my calling to inspire others to have a career they love, culminated in the development of oneTRUEzone.

What is the oneTRUEzone process? It is one that goes well beyond identifying your gift, your calling and your passion. It is a process that involves uncovering how those three elements are interconnected and in sync as it pertains to you and then using that knowledge as a basis for selecting a meaningful career that will lead to personal fulfillment and happiness. The OTZ process will change the life of all who make a commitment to make their lives more meaningful and fulfilling.

When we are aware of our passions, in tune with our calling and cognizant of our own gift, we can discover our true purpose in life and our ideal profession. This knowledge, together with the skills needed to access employment, will enable participants to confidently make prudent, worthwhile decisions regarding their education and will put them on the path to lifelong career happiness and success.

The oneTRUEzone coaching program is designed to help young adults discover what they are meant to do in life; it will help them do what they love and love what they do. As a life coach, motivational speaker, psychotherapist, and financial advisor, I use my knowledge, my personal gifts, and my passion to implement *my* calling, which is to help *others* find the place where work is play.

You can be excited to go to work every day. You can make a living, maybe an amazing one, but when in your oneTRUEzone, you won't even care if you work for free. When your work and you are one and the same, you are motivated to get your day started because it is what excites you most in life. Furthermore, you will be making a difference in the world because your passion is contagious. I am convinced that people who discover and live in their oneTRUEzone have a significant impact on the world.

Admittedly, there are many books and programs that provide career advice. We stand apart because our program transcends merely finding a career that just interests you. It goes way beyond. Our process concentrates wholly on getting to the heart of who you are, the heart of what matters to you. It focuses on getting to the core of your passion, to your one true gift, to your calling. Your "aha moment" will change you forever!

The oneTRUEzone process utilizes a specialized combination of exercises, done individually and in small groups, which enables participants to embark on a meaningful journey of self-exploration toward discovering their one true gift. Through exercises and personal coaching within the oneTRUEzone program, participants arrive at their true destination, one they may have never thought possible.

Always be yourself, express yourself, have faith in yourself; do not go out and look for a successful personality and duplicate it.

~ Bruce Lee

******

An Educator's Perspective

You will recognize your own path when you come upon it, because you will suddenly have all the energy and imagination you will ever need.

~ Jerry Gillies

About Dr. Diane Mitchell

Dr. Diane Mitchell is the curriculum designer and consultant for oneTRUEzone. She brings to the program a diverse and extensive background in education, having taught at the elementary, secondary and college levels. Now a middle-school principal in the Clarkstown Central School District in New York, Diane holds a bachelor of science degree in elementary education from the State University of New York at Oneonta, a master's degree in special education from Fordham University, and a doctoral degree from St. John's University in educational leadership. Diane has published several articles on students' learning styles and their implications for education.

Diane resides in Rockland County, New York, with her husband and three sons and enjoys running marathons. She discovered that her gift is creating educational alternatives, which is what brought her to oneTRUEzone.

Dr. Mitchell and oneTRUEZone

My participation in oneTRUEzone evolved from personal experience with my own three children, as well as my professional work with high school and college young adults as they muddle their way through the process of selecting which college to attend, what they plan to study once there, and their eventual career choice. As both parent and educator, I have always supported my high school and college students by focusing on their academic preparation for college. I encouraged them to take challenging courses and be involved in extra-curricular activities in the arts, athletics and service areas.

As they considered colleges and career options, our conversations revolved around their interests and abilities related to their course work and activities. The school counselors took the same approach. I was fortunate in that I knew from the time I was fifteen years old that I wanted to be an educator. My experiences served as a validation that teaching was the correct and only career option for me because I was so certain that this was what I meant to do. Consequently, I assumed the same would and should hold true for every student.

I first learned of the concept of the "gift" through conversations with Helene over the course of a number of years as she read and researched the ideas for what would eventually develop into the premise of oneTRUEzone. During the same period of time, I had been doing my own research on how environmental, perceptual, social and learning modalities impact a student's academic achievement. My research revealed that every student has a distinctive set of conditions under which they best learn and that those conditions are not always consistent with the way we design our schools and classrooms. This incompatibility can lead to frustration and underachievement on a student's part.

As I learned about the concepts of the gift, calling and passion and how, when students are able to identify each of these factors, they can be successful in following a career path for which they are destined, I was struck by the parallels to my own research with learning styles. As an educator, I knew that the concepts that are the foundation for oneTRUEzone had to be presented in a manner that was appropriate for the young-adult learner. The curriculum for the course was written utilizing research-based strategies that allow each student an individualized pathway to learning, thereby keeping their motivation and interest at an optimal level.

The processes currently used to enable our young adults to make one of the most significant decisions of their lives, their career choice, is contrary to how the influential adults in a child's life approach just about every other educational or social experience. We teach toddlers to speak and behave appropriately by talking to them, modeling behaviors, constant repetition and reinforcement. Parents take their young children to play groups and preschool so they have the opportunity to develop their educational and social skills through interaction with adults and other children their own age.

As children enter school, our classrooms provide various opportunities for students to learn, process and internalize new ideas and concepts. Curriculum is purposely laid out so students revisit and review key concepts over time. Teachers know the value of classroom discussions, cooperative group work, guided practice, and independent work as methods for getting students to understand information. These same proven principles of learning are employed on the ball field, in the dance studio, or at a music lesson.

Students need a knowledgeable adult, be it a teacher, coach or mentor, to orchestrate and oversee their learning. They need repeated opportunities to practice their skills individually and with their peers. Certainly, it would be less expensive if we could simply give students a book to read on their own or a computer program to do, but this independent study, this "figure it out on your own" method, is not successful with most students.

Unfortunately, this is the primary method used by students to pick a career. If statistics regarding the percentage of people dissatisfied in their career are going to change, we as a society need to recognize that a shift is needed in how we prepare our students to make decisions regarding college majors and career choice. We can no longer allow the process to be haphazard and continue to expect students to figure it out on their own.

The oneTRUEzone program was created to right this wrong.

Dr. Diane Mitchell
Curriculum Consultant

Own Your Zone!
Find Your "Sweet Spot"

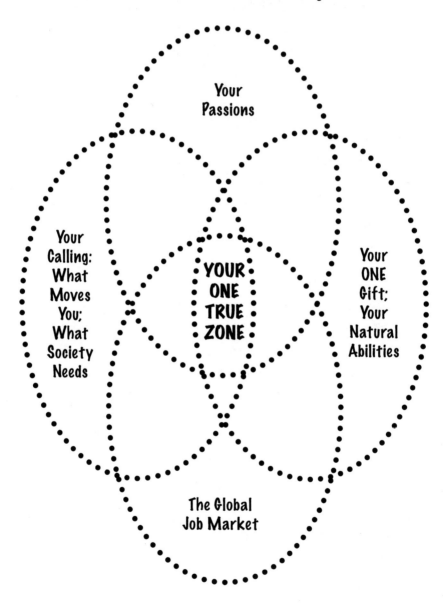

Learn More about oneTRUEzone

Are you anxious about the college-selection process? Are you nervous that your child has not selected a major? Learn from oneTRUEzone founder Helene Naftali how students can discover their gifts and put their uniqueness to work as they chart their higher education and career paths. We offer many types of programs to suit your specific needs. Call us now and oneTRUEzone can be your GPS to uncover your student's gift.

Let Helene Naftali Energize Your Next Event with

Her "Own Your Zone" Seminar or Workshop!

- **Workshops for Parents:** Are you frustrated watching your child struggle in their transition from high school to college or from college to career?

- **Workshops for Students:** Do you feel like you are just spinning your wheels in college? Do you know where you want your education to take you?

- **Workshops for High School or College Educators:** Is the current process of helping students just not enough to guide students into a long-lasting, fulfilling career?

Helene is a dynamic speaker and is available to speak at your next conference, meeting, or group event. Contact us now for more information or to book a speaking engagement, workshop, or other oneTRUEzone event:

oneTRUEzone, P.O. Box 36, Wyckoff, NJ 07481

201-870-0320

www.onetruezone.com

Facebook: /One-True-Zone

Twitter: @onetruezome

Helene on LinkedIn Helene Naftali

ACKNOWLEDGEMENTS

I have the good fortune to know great people whom I truly admire for their vision and understanding of higher education. This book would not have been possible without the support and encouragement from these very important people in my life.

Thank you to...

Dr. Diane Mitchell, curriculum designer and consultant for oneTRUEzone, for keeping me true to our goals and messages and for sharing her insights, expertise and extensive knowledge.

Sara Himeles for all her significant contributions in researching, drafting and helping organize our ideas and messages. Her imprint was vital to our success.

Nanette Fridman for her professional advice and assistance, for continuing to strategically move our team forward, and for believing in me and our cause.

Rena Klosk for her support, editing, researching, recruiting and more, without which we would not have accomplished what we did.

Paul Glen Neuman for his wisdom and experience as an accomplished writer and for helping me to say things more clearly than I could have possibly done on my own.

Sydney Leblanc, who selflessly guided me through this journey to figure out how to get my message across to help young people reach the highest heights possible.

Ken Haman, for selflessly sharing his insights and expertise and for his instinctive ability to see the big picture as well as the details.

Felix Berman for his encouragement and for writing such a great forword for this book.

Mike Mazya for his spontaneous insights and wisdom and for never saying no to any request I had.

Lauren Eichner and Ken Doyle for their coaching and support.

Lisa Summers, for her experience, wisdom and valuable consultations.

My sister, Jody Pflanzer, for her support, encouragement and insights about college-age students and the impact that families have on their decision-making about their lives and careers.

Geri Topfer for being one of my greatest allies and supports and for introducing me to Nanette.

Doug Brown, my dear friend, for his continuous coaching and support through this entire process.

Neil and Barbara Peller for a great editing job and for truly helping to pull it all together.

The parents and other adults we interviewed for allowing me and my team to speak with them and for sharing their challenges, insights, and recommendations. Their stories will inspire young people to get the tools and support they need.*

The college students who have experienced our program or workshops for their testimonials and especially for allowing me to touch their lives through our program. I get to live in *my* one true zone every time I work with them.*

*Participants' names were changed to protect their privacy.

and last, but not least...

My family—my children, Ariel and Taylor, and especially my husband, Paul–for understanding my long days and nights in and out of our home, focused on this book and oneTRUEzone.

Writing this book has truly been a collaborative effort. There are many others whom I would want to thank if space permitted. I appreciate their contributions to my understanding of the ever-changing complexities of higher education, the college experience, and the ways the world and the future for this generation of millennials is changing.

Thank you all for your support!

Helene

END NOTES

1. Rich Karlgaard. "CEO Wisdom Heard From The Top." *Forbes Magazine.* May 27, 2013.

2. Pierre Gergis. "Millennials Are Redefining Work, Corporations Should Take Advantage." April 3, 2013. Retrieved from http://www.forbes.com/sites/calebmelby/2013/04/03/millennials-are-redefining-work-corporations-should-take-advantage/

3. Mel Zuckerman. *Mel's Tips for Healthy Living.* Canyon Ranch Press. June 1, 2011. p. 66.

4. Fifty Lessons, compiler. "W. Howard Lester: Chairman of Williams Sonoma." *Loving Your Work.* Boston: Harvard Business School Press, 2010.

5. Eric Sinoway. "You're Probably Not Very Good at Most Things." HBR Blog Network. October 8, 2012. Retrieved from http://blogs.hbr.org/cs/2012/10/youre_probably_not_very_good_a.html.

6. Rachel Brown. *Temple Times.* Retrieved from http://news.temple.edu/news/conversation-temple-career-guru-rachel-brown May 11, 2009.

7. Peter Gray. "The Decline of Play and the Rise of Psychopathology in Children and Adolescents" *The American Journal of Play.* Spring 2011: p. 444. Retrieved from http://www.psychologytoday.com/files/attachments/1195/ajp-decline-play-published.pdf.

8   Peter Gray. "The Decline of Play and the Rise of Psychopathology in Children and Adolescents" *The American Journal of Play.* Spring 2011. Retrieved from http://www.psychologytoday.com/files/attachments/1195/ajp-decline-play-published.pdf.

9. David Brooks. "It's Not About You." *The New York Times.* May 30, 2011.

10. Mihaly Csikszentmihalyi. Flow: *The Psychology of Optimal Experience.* New York: Harper Collins, 1990.

11. Adam Bryant. "Leadership Never Looks Prepackaged." *The New York Times*. Business Day. August 18, 2012.

12. Adam Bryant. "Mistakes Are O.K., but Never, Ever Lose Your Passion." *The New York Times*. Business Day. October 27, 2012.

13. Phyllis Korkki. "Job Satisfaction vs. a Big Paycheck." *The New York Times*. Jobs. September 11, 2010.

14. Phyllis Korkki. "Job Satisfaction vs. a Big Paycheck." *The New York Times*. Jobs. September 11, 2010.

15. Erin Falconer. "A Letter of Advice to College Freshmen." December 17, 2006. <http://www.pickthebrain.com/blog/a-letter-of-advice-to-college-freshmen/>

16. Rhonda Campbell. "Importance of Loving What You Do as a Creative Small Business Leader." Write Money Incorporated. June 4, 2012. http://www.writemoneyinc.com/2012/06/04/importance-of-loving-what-you-do-as-a-creative-small-business-leader/

17. "Prime Number." *The New York Times*. Week in Review. April 16, 2011.

BIBLIOGRAPHY

"100 Useful Web Tools to Help you Find Your Passion, Calling, or Career."
<http://www.online-college-blog.com/features/100-useful-web-tools-to-help-you-find-your-passion-calling-or-career/>

Ariely, Dan. *The Upside of Irrationality: The Unexpected Benefits of Defying Logic at Work and Home.* New York: Harper Collins, 2010.

Bailey, Simon T. Release Your Brilliance: *The 4 Steps to Transforming Your Life and Revealing Your Genius to the World.* New York, NY: Harper Collins, 2007.

Banks, Sandy. "Look for a Career, Not a Job." 12 June 2010. *Los Angeles Times.*
<http://articles.latimes.com/2010/jun/12/local/la-me-banks-20100612>

Bradberry, Travis. The Personality Code. New York: Putnam Adult, 2007.

Brooks, David. "It's Not About You." *The New York Times.* 30 May 2011.
<http://www.nytimes.com/2011/05/31/opinion/31brooks.html?_r=1&ref=opinion>

Brown, Rachel. *Temple Times.* May 11, 2009.
http://news.temple.edu/news/conversation-temple-career-guru-rachel-brown

Brown, Seth. "Love What You Do and Make Money." *U.S.A. Today.*
<http://usatoday30.usatoday.com/money/books/reviews/2009-03-15-career-renegade_N.htm>

Brown, Traci. "How to Make Money, Have Fun and Love What You Do."
<www.tracibrown.com/How-to-Make-Money-book-index.html>

Bryant, Adam. "In Sports or Business, Always Prepare for the Next Play." *The New York Times,* November 12, 2012.

—. "Leadership Never Looks Prepackaged." *The New York Times.* Business Day. August 18, 2012.

—. "Mistakes Are O,K,, but Never Ever Lose Your Passion." *The New York Times.* October, 2012.

Campbell, Rhonda. "Importance of Loving What You Do as a Creative Small Business Leader." Write Money Incorporated. June 4, 2012. <http://www.writemoneyinc.com/2012/06/04/importance-of-loving-what-you-do-as-a-creative-small-business-leader/>

Cope, Stephen. *The Great Work of Your Life: A Guide for the Journey to Your True Calling.* New York: Bantam, 2012.

Csikszentmihalyi, Mihaly. *Flow: The Psychology of Optimal Experience.* New York: Harper and Row, 1990.

Entin, Esther. "All Work and No Play: Why Your Kids Are More Anxious, Depressed." *The Atlantic.* 12 October 2011. <http://www.theatlantic.com/health/archive/2011/10/all-work-and-no-play-why-your-kids-are-more-anxious-depressed/246422/>

Evanish, Jason. "Why You Should Take Your 20's Seriously." November 1, 2012. <www.jasonevarish.com>

Falconer, Erin. "A Letter of Advice to College Freshmen." Pick the Brain. December 17, 2006. <http://www.pickthebrain.com/blog/a-letter-of-advice-to-college-freshmen/>

"Finding Your Passion." <http://findingyourpassion.org/>

Friedman, Thomas L. "It's P.Q. and C.Q. as Much as I.Q." *The New York Times,* January 29, 2013.

Gergis, Pierre. "Millennials Are Redefining Work, Corporations Should Take Advantage." Forbes.com. April 3, 2013. <http://www.forbes.com/sites/calebmelby/2013/04/03/millennials-are-redefining-work-corporations-should-take-advantage/>

Gray, Peter. "The Decline of Play and the Rise of Psychopathology in Children and Adolescents." *The American Journal of Play.* Spring 2011.

Higson, Phil and Anthony Sturgess. "Goal Setting Tip: Do What You Love." The Happy Manager. <http://www.the-happy-manager.com/articles/goal-setting-tip/>

Karlgaard, Rich. "CEO Wisdom Heard From The Top." *Forbes Magazine.* May 27, 2013.

Korkki, Phyllis. "The Search: Job Satisfaction vs. a Big Paycheck." *The New York Times.* September 11, 2010. <http://www.nytimes.com/2010/09/12/jobs/12search.html>

Markova, Dawna. Wide Open: *On Living With Passion and Purpose.* San Francisco, CA: Conari Press, 2008.

Matheson, Kathy. "Study Tells Students What Their Major is Worth," The Associated Press, May 24, 2011.

Richards, Dick. *Is Your Genius at Work?: 4 Key Questions to Ask Before Your Next Career Move.* Boston, MA: Nicolas Brealey Publishing, 2005.

Robinson, Ken. *The Element: How Finding Your Passion Changes Everything.* New York: Penguin Books, 2009.

Rosengren, Curt. "Why Loving Your Work Matters." *U.S. News.* <http://money.usnews.com/money/blogs/ outside-voices-careers/2011/06/09/why-loving-your-work-matters>

Rowley, Laura. "Money and Happiness: Laura Rowley Helps You Find Both." Daily Finance. <http://www.dailyfinance.com/2011/11/01/ introducing-money-and-happiness-personal-finance-expert-laura/>

Saad, Lydia. "U.S. Workers Least Happy With Their Work Stress and Pay." Gallup Economy. http://www.gallup.com/poll/158723/workers-least-happy-work-stress-pay.aspx

Shafer, Joyce. "What Is Your Gift and Do You Share It?
<http://www.selfgrowth.com/articles/
what_is_your_gift_and_do_you_share_it>

Silverman, Rachel Emma. "Work as Labor or Love?" *The Wall Street Journal,* October 17, 2012.

Stoltz, Paul G., Ph.D. "How to Triple Your Chances of Getting a Job."
<http://jobs.aol.com/articles/2011/06/15/
triple-chances-of-getting-a-job/
?icid=maing-grid7%7Cmain5%7Cdl9%7Csec3_lnk1%7C70853>

Sweeney, Camille and Josh Gosfield, "Secret Ingredient for Success,"
The New York Times, January 19, 2013.

Tierney, John. "A New Gauge to See What's Beyond Happiness." *The New York Times.*
<http://www.nytimes.com/2011/05/17/science/
17tierney.html?pagewanted=1&_r=2&ref=science&>

Winfrey, Oprah. "What Oprah Knows for Sure." Oprah Show.
<http://www.oprah.com/oprahshow/What-Oprah-Knows-For-Sure

Zuckerman, Mel. *Mel's Tips for Healthy Living.* Tuscon, Arizona:
Canyon Ranch Press, 2011.